NEW AND SELECTED POEMS

135,37

Yves Bonnefoy

NEW AND
SELECTED POEMS

Edited by John Naughton
and Anthony Rudolf

THE UNIVERSITY OF
CHICAGO PRESS

The French-language poems in this book are reprinted by permission of Mercure de France and appeared originally as the following: *Du mouvement et de l'immobilité de Douve* © Mercure de France 1953; *Hier régnant désert* © Mercure de France 1958; *Pierre écrite* © Mercure de France 1965; *Dans le leurre du seuil* © Mercure de France 1975; *Ce qui fut sans lumière* © Mercure de France 1987; *Là où retombe la flèche* © Mercure de France 1988; *Début et fin de la neige* © Mercure de France 1991; and the poem "De Vent et de fumée" from *La Vie errante* © Mercure de France 1993.

The English translations of the poems in part I, *Du mouvement et de l'immobilité de Douve,* translated by Galway Kinnell, are reprinted from Yves Bonnefoy, *Early Poems, 1947–1959* (Ohio University Press, 1991). Reprinted with the permission of The Ohio University Press/Swallow Press, Athens, Ohio. The first ten poems and the last poem of part III, *Pierre écrite,* are reprinted from Yves Bonnefoy, *Poems 1959–1975,* translated by Richard Pevear. Translation copyright © 1985 by Random House, Inc. Reprinted by permission of Random House, Inc.

The University of Chicago Press, Chicago 60637
© 1995 by The University of Chicago
All rights reserved. Published 1995
Printed in the United States of America
04 03 02 01 00 99 98 97 96 95   1 2 3 4 5

ISBN: 0-226-06458-1 (cloth)
0-226-06460-3 (paper)

Library of Congress Cataloging-in-Publication Data

Bonnefoy, Yves.
[Poems. English. Selections]
New and selected poems / Yves Bonnefoy ; edited by John Naughton and Anthony Rudolf.
p.   cm.
Includes bibliographical references and index.
1. Bonnefoy, Yves—Translations into English.   I. Naughton, John T.   II. Rudolf, Anthony, 1942–   .   III. Title.
PQ2603.0533A2   1995
841'.914—dc20
95-10350
CIP

CONTENTS

FOREWORD

I

Yves Bonnefoy's poetry has been translated into many European and other languages, and several of his books have been translated into the same language more than once. Over a period of nearly forty years the interest in his work has been so widespread and at the same time so deep that the explanation for this rare phenomenon is a self-explanation, namely that he is a great and necessary poet whose writing, transcending immediate language barriers, speaks directly to a *thou:* each reader, in his or her own solitude, for the time of the poem looks the poet in the eye/I, takes the measure, or measures the take, of a lyrical voice at once intimate and magisterial and then, unwriting himself or herself out of the poem, returns to the world changed by an experience only words can generate but deeper than any word, found beyond telling.

In his eloquent Introduction my coeditor John Naughton deploys his profound knowledge and experience of Bonnefoy's work to guide the reader along the path of the poet's development, focusing on the central concerns of each book in turn. In this foreword I would like to make some informal comments of my own on the work of a poet increasingly ranked with the likes of Paz and Milosz.

In theory and in practice Yves Bonnefoy's six books of poetry are conceived and structured as architectonic wholes. They are artfully orchestrated ensembles that seek to contain and to reconcile opposing forces. Their richness and complexity are inevitably diminished in an anthology such as ours. Even the most intelligently composed selection perpetrates a violence on their intricate design. Nonetheless, beginning in most cases with the complete opening sequence of a book, we have attempted to construct a selection which will yield a coherent sense of Bonnefoy's tone and style, and of the developmentally cyclical leitmotifs within and between books. Our intention and our hope is that readers will find this structure so fascinating and so frustrating that they will seek out complete books in translation and in the original (see bibliography).

An enormous number of single poems have appeared in English translation in literary magazines and anthologies and other books for many years now. We considered the possibility of choosing the best available version of each poem we wanted to include, but decided that since particular translators have over many years concentrated on certain books, the advantages conferred by a more unified tone would outweigh improved local felicities in this or that poem. A minimum of initiative will point the interested reader in the direction of other published versions. It is not without regret on our part and on the part of Yves Bonnefoy that some beautiful translations have had to be excluded in the interests of the best compromise John Naughton and I could negotiate with each other, with Yves Bonnefoy, with the original texts, and with the available translations.

The two major selections of Yves Bonnefoy's prose in English translation—*The Act and the Place of Poetry* and *The Lure and the Truth of Painting*—reveal something of the extraordinary richness and diversity of the poet's thought. For, beyond his verse and his prose poems (also represented in this book), Bonnefoy has generated a unique and remarkable ongoing meditation on the Western tradition in art and literature—a tradition now in crisis. Consubstantial with his poetry, this meditation displays a complexity of thought and a mighty erudition, which, however, do not swamp the general reader, thanks both to the author's unrivaled dialectical intelligence and to his constant return to the simple things of the world.

Is there another poet alive who is engaged in such an ambitious prose project? Paz, Milosz, Herbert, Enzensberger are all authors of important prose books, but they and others have not sought to integrate a transnational tradition, and for very good historical reasons of their own unmaking, their own unwriting. Down another road, many major poets, Char, Frénaud, Jabès—to instance Bonnefoy's immediate elders in France, as well as his friend and contemporary Celan—have produced virtually no "second" oeuvre. Perhaps the nearest parallels to Yves Bonnefoy's re-statement and redefinition of our heritage can be found in the second oeuvres of Eliot, Breton, and Laura Riding. Had Osip Mandelstam lived . . .

II

The translation of poetry, especially that of a living poet, and most particularly that of one you have come to know as a friend, emerges from an extraordinarily intimate and personal matrix. For that very reason it must at the same time generate a radix of unsentimental control and radical otherness. Yves Bonnefoy's second book, *Hier régnant désert*, found me in a Cambridge bookshop in 1963, when I was twenty-one. I began reading it, and my life was changed, changed because, to start with, I knew it *would* be changed. An affinity was elected, a promise was redeemed—a promise hitherto buried in the undifferentiated and diffuse soul of a student in love with the idea of poetry. I had a guide, a master. Henceforth there would be a life in writing. Fortunately, Bonnefoy, man and poet, negates the very idea of guru. There are no answers. A root is planted in the womb, and spiritual awareness is born. From such awareness the route of personal salvation is plotted: begin where you find yourself, build your own community through the word, then unwrite yourself out of the poem—to "broken bread" and "simple stone," to "ripe fruits" and "transhumant stars," to "a fire caught sight of in the sudden night,/like the table glimpsed in a poor house."

I have never stopped reading *Hier régnant désert* (nor the other books), translation itself being the most intense form of reading imaginable. I made my first translations of Yves Bonnefoy's poems in the first few days, months, and years after my bookshop discov-ery, during which time I was also attempting to write my own early poems. Bonnefoy himself, already well versed in the English language, made some very helpful suggestions about my transla-tions of his work, but always and rightly insisted that the last word belongs to the translator. Kind intermediaries organized publica-tion of the early translations in 1968. I will risk saying now that I am mightily relieved to have been able to publish revised versions in 1985 and further revised versions for this selection. One day I hope to publish complete versions of *Hier régnant désert* and *Douve*. Meanwhile, despite my embarrassment about some of those early versions, the memory of reading this great poet in my quondam condition of radical innocence and grace ("the sad place of a song I carried") will remain with me forever. "Listen, I come to life again in these forests/under the leaves of memory."

All readers must be grateful that Bonnefoy's "gravité enflammée," in the fine phrase of Philippe Jaccottet, continues to reveal itself in poem, in prose poem and in prose. At a time of deep spiritual and material crisis in our only world, a twofold crisis symbolized by the environmental degradation of those forests and rivers of Europe that have inspired poets for centuries, Bonnefoy's constant and apparently paradoxical demand that we unwrite ourselves out of the text and return to the world which we hold in trust for our children—with the implicit responsibility to repair it—is a proud and vital demonstration of the continuing relevance of art in our lives. Surely Yves Bonnefoy was present in spirit when Celan visited Heidegger in the Black Forest.

The esperance which wrestles with despair and wins over that worthy opponent is the special gift of great poets: there is a line which runs from Hölderlin through Rilke to Seferis and Celan— and to Yves Bonnefoy, on his "horizon of a voice where stars are falling,/moon merging with the chaos of the dead."

ANTHONY RUDOLF

INTRODUCTION

About forty years ago, when he was not yet thirty, Yves Bonnefoy wrote the following lines:

> *La lumière profonde a besoin pour paraître*
> *D'une terre rouée et craquante de nuit.*
> *C'est d'un bois ténébreux que la flamme s'exalte.*
> *Il faut à la parole même une matière,*
> *Un inerte rivage au-delà de tout chant.*
>
> *Il te faudra franchir la mort pour que tu vives,*
> *La plus pure présence est un sang répandu.*

> If it is to appear, the deep light needs
> A ravaged soil cracking with night.
> It is from the dark wood that the flame will leap.
> Speech itself needs such substance,
> A lifeless shore beyond all singing.
>
> You will have to go through death to live,
> The purest presence is blood which is shed.

And it is true that all his work is marked by the interplay of light and darkness. No affirmation ever emerges except through the recognition of limitation and defeat. Indeed, the poetry of Yves Bonnefoy is always a dialogue, a "theater" in which joyful celebration of earth's simple blessings must confront the ever-present awareness of futility and death. His poetry is often like the light in the paintings of Poussin or Constable that appears in the breaks between ominous black clouds.

■   ■   ■

Born in Tours in 1923, Bonnefoy was, like Rimbaud, whom he reveres, a brilliant young student, graduating with honors from the

Lycée Descartes. Like Rimbaud, too, Bonnefoy lost his father—a worker whose job involved assembling locomotives—at an early age. After his father's death, his mother took a job as a teacher at a grade school outside Tours and looked after the education of her son. Bonnefoy eventually received an advanced degree in mathematics and philosophy before coming to occupied Paris in 1944. There, he became involved in the surrealist circles, met André Breton, and edited his own small review, called, with appropriate iconoclasm, *La Révolution la nuit*. He also married, and he taught mathematics and science for a time. The publication in 1953 of his first major book of poetry, *Du mouvement et de l'immobilité de Douve* (*On the Motion and Immobility of Douve*)—the work from which the above lines are quoted—immediately put him at the forefront of the new generation of French poets. Five other books of poetry have since appeared—*Hier régnant désert* (*Yesterday's Desert Dominion; 1958*), *Pierre écrite* (*Words in Stone; 1965*), *Dans le leurre du seuil* (*In the Lure of the Threshold; 1975*), *Ce qui fut sans lumière* (*In the Shadow's Light; 1987*), *Début et fin de la neige* (*The Beginning and the End of the Snow; 1991*)—as well as translations of most of Shakespeare's major plays and selected poems of Donne, Keats, and Yeats. Bonnefoy's election to the Collège de France in 1981 (to fill the seat vacated by the death of Roland Barthes) gave official recognition to a supremely, if quietly, distinguished career. In addition to his poetry and translations, Yves Bonnefoy has also steadily produced a body of remarkable criticism, comparable in its range and importance to Baudelaire's critical works or to Valéry's *Variétés*: reflections on the act and place of poetry, on the visual arts and their relation to poetry, on Shakespeare and the English poetic tradition, on the problems and rewards of translating.

■　■　■

Bonnefoy spent the summers of his youth at his grandfather's house in Toirac, near the Lot river. The moments spent there in the atemporality of an ever-repeated summer were decisive in the development of the young boy's sensibility. "I found this country beautiful," he has said. "It even formed me in my deepest choices, with its vast, deserted plateaus and gray stone, and its rainstorms, which sometimes lasted for days, above the closed-up chateaus."

On the other hand, he remembers the provincial city of Tours as being, in those days, a place "where what didn't attract attention, where what was perpetuated without any real becoming, and without unsettling any established habit, was the law." It was the subversion of this conventional and routine vision of life that first incited Bonnefoy's interest in surrealism. Drawn to the movement's desire to see the world in a fresh and revolutionary way, stirred by its attraction to fleeting and seemingly insignificant dimensions of everyday life, he was, however, put off by the occultist tendencies that animated it on other levels, and by its seeming faith in hidden or secret powers. The object, freed from the conceptual or "everyday" thinking that merely categorizes it absentmindedly, is indeed a *presence,* in Bonnefoy's view. But the surrealist tendency to present things as devoid of meaningful context, as set off against nothingness and absence, creates, in his opinion, a kind of spectral or demonic presence, a negative luminosity—whereas it is the richness and unity of being that true presences should reveal. "It is this unity," Bonnefoy has said, "that asks us to give ourselves with trust to finitude, because there is no totality except in the mutual recognition of each of the parts that make up the whole, and this recognition has limitation as its essence, but a limitation that earns us the right, through the very assumption of our nothingness, to accede to the universal." Thus the surrealist image, because it is offered in a way that seems indifferent to the realities of time, space, causality, and to the laws of nature and being, "subverts the principles that allow us to decipher the world." Recognition of our finitude—of our place in time, of the role of chance in human destiny, of mortality—is an existential starting point, since this recognition unites us with others who share the same fate, and since in moments of extreme illumination this awareness allows us to perceive the greater unity in which all finite things participate. And so it is that Bonnefoy places as epigraph to *Du mouvement et de l'immobilité de Douve* a citation from Hegel that in fact orients all his thinking and animates his poetry from the earliest texts to the most recent: "But the life of the spirit is not frightened at death and does not keep itself pure of it. It endures death and maintains itself in it."

The publication of *Douve* was greeted with almost unanimous critical enthusiasm and approval. Here was a voice, as even the somewhat resistant Jean Grosjean admitted, to be listened to with the gravest attention. Inevitably, the question was raised: Who or what is Douve? A mysterious feminine presence, her death, physical decomposition, and resurrection put one in mind of the romantic notion enunciated by Edgar Allan Poe that "the death . . . of a beautiful woman is, unquestionably, the most poetic topic in the world." And her relation to the poetic narrator would seem also to support Poe's conviction that "the lips best suited for such topic are those of a bereaved lover."

On the other hand, she seems intimately related to the poetic process itself, to the nature of inspiration and to the impact of death on inspiration. Now, death is a category in this poem which involves recognition not only of the fate of flesh but also of the inertia and lifelessness of established representation. The constant resurrections of Douve, her almost Ovidian metamorphoses, are the poetic expression of the recurrent but ephemeral moment of epiphanous vision, which retreats from what would try to express it. Poetic utterance is not equal to the reality it seeks to articulate; what it touches dies from its touch—only to be resurrected as an unreachable domain, inexhaustible and eternally elusive. (The French word *douve* means a "moat" or a "ditch.") On the other hand, poetry's refusal to resign itself to the impossible is the reminder that Douve is associated with human spirit, with those spiritual aspirations suggested by the English word "dove"—the traditional symbol of the Holy Spirit.

Death founds true discourse. This has been the poet's central conviction from the outset, as is made clear in *Douve* through the beautiful poem called "Vrai Corps" ("True Body").

> *Close la bouche et lavé le visage,*
> *Purifié le corps, enseveli*
> *Ce destin éclairant dans la terre du verbe,*
> *Et le mariage le plus bas s'est accompli.*
>
> *Tue cette voix qui criait à ma face*
> *Que nous étions hagards et séparés,*
> *Murés ces yeux: et je tiens Douve morte*
> *Dans l'âpreté de soi avec moi refermée.*

Et si grand soit le froid qui monte de ton être,
Si brûlant soit le gel de notre intimité,
Douve, je parle en toi; et je t'enserre
Dans l'acte de connaître et de nommer.

The mouth shut tight, the face washed,
The body purified, that shining fate
Buried in the earth of words,
And the most basic marriage is accomplished.

Silenced that voice which shouted to my face
That we were stranded and apart,
Walled up those eyes: and I hold Douve dead
In the rasping self locked with me again.

And however great the coldness rising from you,
However searing the ice of our embrace,
Douve, I do speak in you; and I clasp you
In the act of knowing and of naming.

The destiny of death is clarifying for the poet. Although a humbling recognition for the proud head, for the intellectual constructions of men, which are elaborated outside the fatalities of time and chance, the awareness of death is espoused here in an act of intimacy, of marriage with consciousness, having for consequence that subjectivity will henceforth speak from the context of a new vision, a new orientation. The verbs *tenir* ("to hold"), *refermer* ("to shut in"), and *enserrer* ("to clasp," "to embrace," "to hold close") all emphasize a voluntary adhesion to the principle of death, seen as a necessary component of both a just appreciation of one's being-in-the-world and the poetic act which would take honest stock of this situation—that is, of knowing and naming.

In this sense, a true recognition of death is the proper baptismal experience for poetic consciousness. It is Paul Claudel's notion of "knowing" that Bonnefoy is echoing here, and this is only one in a whole network of such reference to French poetic history and convention that animates the poem. The idea is that the poet comes to birth with (*co-naître*) what he knows (*connaître*) through naming it. The dead Douve becomes the apparition of the living Dove who is discovered to an awakened consciousness—at once an illumination of finality and a call to authentic poetic orientation. A strange voice will speak of this impersonally and with a kind of incantatory conviction on more than one occasion in *Douve*.

> *Que saisir sinon qui s'échappe,*
> *Que voir sinon qui s'obscurcit,*
> *Que désirer sinon qui meurt,*
> *Sinon qui parle et se déchire?*

> What can be seized except what escapes,
> What can be seen except what grows dark,
> What can be desired except what dies,
> Except what speaks and is torn asunder?

It would be a mistake, I think, to isolate Yves Bonnefoy from his historical moment. His essays on Shakespeare focus on the fascination in Shakespeare's work with the "weakening of that faith in the meaning of the world that ensured the survival of society" and stress the fact that this is the obsessional center around which his entire opus turns. Something of the same sort could be said of Bonnefoy himself, since the search for meaning in a world where it seems to have vanished completely is surely at the heart of his enterprise. Thus, despite his repeated acknowledgment that he belongs to a generation that "comes after the gods," that his starting point is in the recognition of the definitive collapse of traditional systems of value and sacred order, Bonnefoy's idea of poetry is inseparable from a certain form of affirmation and hopefulness. "I should like to bring together, almost identify poetry and hope," he wrote in 1959. But hopefulness, in order to be real and not purely illusory, must situate itself in the midst of the realities of the human condition—which is to say, in the very heart of the restrictions that bear upon us from all sides.

Gaëtan Picon, writing of the new French poets who had emerged after World War II, said of them that they felt totally disinherited from all poetic tradition. Marked by war, by a history "so monstrous that it denies all poetic possibility," the new generation of poets, in Picon's view, felt itself "separated from the word it might be, from the universe it might name." Appropriately, Picon placed the efforts of the new poets "between the fact of ruin and the desire for reconstruction." Some of these notions may be felt in certain of the poems of *Douve*.

> *Ainsi marcherons-nous sur les ruines d'un ciel immense,*
> *Le site au loin s'accomplira*
> *Comme un destin dans la vive lumière.*

> *Le pays le plus beau longtemps cherché*
> *S'étendra devant nous terre des salamandres.*

> *Regarde, diras-tu, cette pierre:*
> *Elle porte la présence de la mort.*
> *Lampe secrète c'est elle qui brûle sous nos gestes,*
> *Ainsi marchons-nous éclairés.*

> So we will walk on the ruins of a vast sky,
> The far-off landscape will bloom
> Like a destiny in the vivid light.

> The long-sought most beautiful country
> Will lie before us, land of salamanders.

> Look, you will say, at this stone:
> Death shines from it.
> Secret lamp it is this that burns under our steps,
> Thus we walk lighted.

The first line, on one level at least, seems to speak of a painful period of decline—the end of a certain idealist tradition, the repudiation of the now invalid images of romantic reveries. The heavens which have collapsed with their images represent precisely the infinite imaginary which is the extreme form of alienation. On the other hand, the "ruins" of the first line of the poem already point to the guiding stone which will appear at the end of the text.

The future tense of the verb is suggestive of the search or quest for meaning in an age of spiritual eclipse. The "site" of which the poem speaks indicates the ground upon which the future dwelling will be established. This ground is the land of the salamander, spirit of resurrection, survivor of fire and flood, and symbol for Bonnefoy, through its silent, unpretentious adherence to earth, of "all that is pure." This land, which a misguided longing may have "sought" unknowingly, is perhaps nothing so much as the simple evidence before us, its most common features—water, stone, tree—improbable and completely sustaining presences for the vision purified of an unbounded nostalgia, or, put another way, infused with the energy normally expended on transcendence and dream.

The exhortation of the last stanza is the poet's determination to convert the futurity of the projected quest of the first two parts of the poem into a present apprehension of both limitation and plenitude. This intuition is granted, as it so often is in Bonnefoy's work, by the stone. Bonnefoy's stones are reminiscent of those sepulchers in Poussin's *Et in Arcadia Ego* pictures, which rise up as a reminder of death's presence even in Arcadia to control an absentminded absorption in nature's splendors; they have something, too, of those skulls in Georges de la Tour that seem, more than the light from the nearby candle, to be the real source of the illumination on the penitent's face. Recognition of finitude is the "secret" source of grounding and orientation in the poem. It is what now illuminates the poetic effort, the act of "knowing and naming." The lamp of stone will accompany the poet through all his future wanderings, casting a dark but unmistakable light along his path.

■ ■ ■

Douve works out a shattering death rite. But if it deals in destruction, if it seeks to shatter the safe enclosures provided by representation and idea, if it means to restore us to a primitive sense of mystery and awe, it does so largely in a mythic, atemporal setting. In short, while the poem sets out to record the devastations of being and the travail of becoming, it does so without incorporating a sense of existential time, or of the poet's own specific place in it. The next book of poems, *Hier régnant désert,* will mark this crisis of consciousness.

Few modern poems will have registered a more absolute impression of stagnation than the one provided in the opening pages of Bonnefoy's second book of poetry. The collection clearly reflects more suffering and self-doubt than do any of Bonnefoy's other works. It is also the most painfully self-conscious. Interrogation of methods, the effort to constitute a "self," the struggle with the question of time, the search for artistic values, for new departure—the problems which pervade *Hier régnant désert* constitute the difficult coming of age of the poet and translate his struggle to establish both a poetic and an ethical identity.

Had Bonnefoy discovered after the profoundly searching recognition of death in *Douve* that outside of its articulation in a formal system, mortality, our passage through duration to inevitable extinction, has a more paralyzing and less easily mastered dimension than he might have hoped when he was in his twenties? Here is the poet *nel mezzo del camin,* in a state of apathy and inertia, perhaps calling his very sincerity into question, separated from his deepest self, in the grip of what the medieval world knew as *acedia,* recoiling from spiritual imperatives. In his autobiographical work, *L'Arrière-pays* (*Heartland*), Bonnefoy provides an analysis of his state of mind at the time of *Hier régnant désert*. He had fallen, he says, "into the unremitting sorrow of dream and inhibition with regard to it." "In fact," he goes on to say, "what I accused in myself, what I thought I could recognize and judge, was the pleasure of creating artistically, the preference given to created beauty over lived experience. I saw correctly that such a choice, in devoting words to themselves, in making of them a private language, created a universe which guaranteed the poet *everything;* except that by withdrawing from the openness of days, by disregarding time and other people, he was in fact headed toward nothing except solitude." This judgment in part explains the repeated attacks on formal beauty that are found in this work, as for instance in the poem called "Imperfection Is the Summit."

> *Il y avait qu'il fallait détruire et détruire et détruire,*
> *Il y avait que le salut n'est qu'à ce prix.*
>
> *Ruiner la face nue qui monte dans le marbre,*
> *Marteler toute forme toute beauté.*
>
> *Aimer la perfection parce qu'elle est le seuil,*
> *Mais la nier sitôt connue, l'oublier morte,*
>
> *L'imperfection est la cime.*

There was this:
You had to destroy, destroy, destroy.
There was this:
Salvation is only found at such a price.

You had to
Ruin the naked face that rises in the marble,
Hammer at every beauty every form.

Love perfection because it is the threshold,
But deny it once known, once dead forget it.

Imperfection is the summit.

As is the case in all of Bonnefoy's poetical works—and their moral dimension resides in this—*Hier régnant désert* seeks to master the problems it presents and to balance one set of forces with another. The painful awareness of entrapment in a dark night of the soul ("I was lost in the silence I gave birth to") is the first step toward that new dawn constantly invoked throughout the poem. Awareness of one's past, of the nightmare-haunted child one has been, may initiate a process of transformation, as Bonnefoy has so movingly put it in his analysis of Rimbaud, through which "*ardent patience . . .* will change what one endures into what one takes on, suffering into being; those 'dead bodies which will be judged" into the vigilance of which we have always been capable and whose truth dawn will see firmly established in an existence which begins anew." The entire movement of the poem is to reconnect with that dawn which is "the daughter of tears," and to restore "the footstep to its true place." The radiantly confident poems that end the book, inspired in part by a trip the poet made to Greece, are a sign of this renewed self-mastery.

> *Ici l'inquiète voix consent d'aimer*
> *La pierre simple.*
> *Les dalles que le temps asservit et délivre,*
> *L'olivier dont la force a goût de sèche pierre.*

> Here the unquiet voice agrees to love
> Simple stone,
> Flagstones time enslaves, delivers,
> The olive tree whose strength tastes of dry stone.

. . .

If Yves Bonnefoy's first two books of poetry are marked by a solitary and stoical vigilance, by an icy sleeplessness and constriction, his third book, *Pierre écrite,* published in 1965, is striking precisely because of its contrasting expansiveness and trust, and because of the sudden presence of a beloved other who appears—"smiling, pristine, sea-washed"—like some Venus from her shell, and whose "frail earthly hands" untangle "the sorrowful knot of dreams." How do we explain the new fullness and confidence of this book? Why can the poet now exclaim:

> *Nous n'avons plus besoin*
> *D'images déchirantes pour aimer.*
> *Cet arbre nous suffit, là-bas . . .*

> We no longer need
> Rending images to love.
> That tree over there is enough . . .

Part of the explanation undoubtedly lies in the maturation on which the poems repeatedly insist. In an important essay on Shakespeare called "Readiness, Ripeness: *Hamlet, Lear,*" Bonnefoy remarks that Hamlet confronts a world without meaning and hence feels that "a single act still has some logic and is worthy of being carried out: and that is to take great pains to detach oneself from every illusion and to be ready to accept everything—everything, but first of all and especially death, essence of all life—with irony and indifference." The "ripeness" that is so often apparent in *King Lear* reflects "the quintessence of the world's order, whose unity one seems to breathe," whereas the "readiness" of Hamlet is "the reverse side of this order, when one no longer sees anything in the grayness of the passing days but the incomprehensible weave." One might characterize *Hier régnant désert*—surely Bonnefoy's "grayest" work—as a kind of Hamlet-phase, or Hamlet-crisis. The epigraph Bonnefoy chooses for *Pierre écrite,* on the other hand, is a quotation from *The Winter's Tale*—that play which Bonnefoy sees as "in fact solar" and which he feels could be "superimposed on *Hamlet* point for point": "Thou mettest with things dying; I with things newborn." Indeed, the new collection, with its rich and colorful evocations of nature and place, of languorous erotic experience, of the blessings of domestic life, does seem to constitute a fresh departure for the poet.

In the early nineteen-sixties, Bonnefoy and his American wife, Lucy Vines, discovered an abandoned building in Provence, near the Vachère mountain, a building which at one time had been a monastery, and which, after the Revolution, had been converted into some kind of farmhouse. Bonnefoy's attachment to the place and to the surrounding countryside was instantaneous. It was here that he felt that he must live.

> Wooded hills, a vast sky, narrow paths that run among the stones beneath red clouds, the eternity of the simple rural life, the few shepherds, the flocks of sheep, silence everywhere: only Virgil or Poussin, whom I loved so much, had spoken to me seriously of these things. . . . This was the beginning of several years of profound attachment, despite great difficulties, and even a sense of contradiction that was painful to experience. We got rid of the hay and the partitions that the peasants had added after the Revolution to reduce the size of the rooms, and thus, thanks to our efforts, the religious character of what once had been the church was restored, but its authority scarcely lent itself to the daily life we had to lead, even though we tried—in vain of course—to bring this life as close as possible to the being of the snake beneath the stones of the entrance, or the buzzards and the owls and the hoopoes that built their nests in the walls or in the open barns. There was more of the real here than anywhere else, more immanence in the light on the angle of the walls or in the water from new storms, but there were also a thousand forms of impossibility—I won't go into all the turns this took—and so there was also more dreaming.

This place is the central element in all of Bonnefoy's poetry from the early nineteen-sixties until the present. It is the heart of *Pierre écrite* and of *Dans le leurre du seuil* (1975), and its memory haunts the recent *Ce qui fut sans lumière* (1987). It is not, to be sure, as though the poet had forgotten about finitude. A number of the poems that make up the second section of *Pierre écrite* are simply called "A Stone," and they may be read as epitaphs on tombstones that recall the brevity or futility of human existence. Still, what emerges predominantly in this work is the sense of affirmation and peace, and the feeling of life being shared. Though death is ever present, even in the place that seems the gateway to unity and plenitude, it is made to share a place with "the wisdom that chooses living," as the following poem, called simply "A Voice," makes clear.

> Nous vieillissions, lui le feuillage et moi la source,
> Lui le peu de soleil et moi la profondeur,
> Et lui la mort et moi la sagesse de vivre.
>
> J'acceptais que le temps nous présentât dans l'ombre
> Son visage de faune au rire non moqueur,
> J'aimais que se levât le vent qui porte l'ombre
>
> Et que mourir ne fût en obscure fontaine
> Que troubler l'eau sans fond que le lierre buvait.
> J'aimais, j'étais debout dans le songe éternel.

> We grew old, he the leaves and I the pool,
> He a patch of sunlight and I the depths,
> He death and I the wisdom that chose life.
>
> I consented that time would show us in the dark
> His faun's face with its unmocking laugh,
> I was glad that the dark-bearing wind would rise
>
> And that dying was but a slight troubling
> Of the fathomless water where the ivy drank.
> I was glad, I stood in the eternal dream.

The opening emphasis on aging contributes to the sense of an ongoing and maturing relationship in which recognition of death and limitation is diffused through a tempered acceptance of life. The insistence upon gladness and love point to a change in vision, to that "change in the light" of which another poem speaks.

> Nous ne nous voyons plus dans la même lumière,
> Nous n'avons plus les mêmes yeux, les mêmes mains.
> L'arbre est plus proche, et la voix des sources plus vive,
> Nos pas sont plus profonds, parmi les morts.

We see each other now in a different light,
Our eyes, our hands, will never be the same.
The tree is closer, sharper the voice of springs,
Our steps are deeper too, among the dead.

■　■　■

Pierre écrite ends on a note of provisional triumph: vision has been purified, changed, "dredged from night," as the last poem puts it. Bonnefoy's next book, *Dans le leurre du seuil,* published ten years later, reflects this change, since the work is quite different from anything published earlier. The longest, densest, most complex of all of Bonnefoy's poems, *Dans le leurre du seuil* is the poet's *summa,* which gives dramatic expression to the concerns of a lifetime: the search for place, the desire for transcendence, the meditation on death and the act of writing, on the role and status of the image. Divided into seven sections of varying lengths, the work has a continuous narrative flow which distinguishes it from the previous collections, although these too, I think it could be shown, have their own deeply buried narrative line. Once again, the poem is set in the house in Provence. The dwelling, with its gaping holes and missing stones, with its need for mending and restoration, becomes the symbol of a menaced but indomitable sacred order, the persistence of which the poet sees reflected in the simple, daily realities surrounding him.

The poem begins during a sleepless, doubt-filled night. The poet remembers the strange death of his friend, the musicologist Boris de Schloezer. What had he seen at the moment of crossing the awesome threshold? What was he coming to understand, to accept?

> *Il écouta, longtemps,*
> *Puis il se redressa, le feu*
> *De cette oeuvre qui atteignait,*
> *Qui sait, à une cime*
> *De déliements, de retrouvailles, de joie*
> *Illumina son visage.*

He listened for a long time,
Then drew himself up, the fire
Of that work which reached,
Who knows, some pinnacle
Of release, of reunion, of joy
Lit up his face.

This transfigured vision reminds the poet of a painted image, doubtless of the Poussin painting on *The Finding of Moses,* which is now in the Louvre. The picture seems to evoke a world of peaceful harmony and even breathing, where mind and world are in perfect accord. It is as though longing had been dispersed in the real, and dreams dispelled to allow a simple evidence to emerge in the form of a child. The images in the painting—the boatman, the rescued infant, the Pharoah's daughter—animate a whole network of verbal associations in Bonnefoy's poem.

The second section of the poem is a summons to the will to combat the seeming futility of the world. Then, in the following sections, the poet returns to the bed he has left and thus initiates the process by means of which he comes to participate in the kind of miraculously affirmative vision his friend has enjoyed and which he sees reflected both in Poussin's painting and in Shakespeare's *The Winter's Tale,* through the figure of Hermione, reanimated from the frozen immobility to which possessiveness and suspicion have reduced her. Parts three and four of the poem evoke the process of conception. But it is a characteristic of Bonnefoy's work to place erotic experience in the context of the vaster workings of nature and to present it as metaphorical of the search for marriage in writing between the word and the real. He therefore deals with the question of *generation* on both the biological and the spiritual levels. The future child promises a new and joyful world, less tortured and rent, and is therefore both infant and sign—the force that "carries the world."

Oui, par l'enfant

Et par ces quelques mots que j'ai sauvés
Pour une bouche enfante. "Vois, le serpent

Du fond de ce jardin ne quitte guère
L'ombre fade du buis. Tous ses désirs
Sont de silence et de sommeil parmi les pierres.
La douleur de nommer parmi les choses
Finira." C'est déjà musique dans l'épaule,
Musique dans le bras qui la protège,
Parole sur des lèvres reconciliées.

Yes, by the child

And by these few words I saved
For a child's mouth. "Look, the serpent
At the back of the garden hardly ever leaves
The lusterless shade of the box-tree. His only desire
Is for silence and sleep among the stones.
The painfulness of naming among things
Will cease." There is already music in the shoulder,
Music in the arm that protects it,
Words on lips that have been reconciled.

The fifth section of the book, called "The Earth," which is published here in its entirety, is the first movement of the vigorous acceptance and affirmative certainty which characterize the last three sections of the poem.

■ ■ ■

Reading the last sections of *Dans le leurre du seuil,* one might have been tempted to think that Bonnefoy had arrived at a level of acceptance and serenity that made more writing unnecessary. And it is true that his first four books are a kind of theater of self-knowing, in which the difficult struggle for self-mastery is played out, and to a certain extent achieved. A more recent work, *Ce qui fut sans lumière,* published twelve years after *Dans le leurre du seuil,* makes it clear, however, that the poet had yet another kind of drama to face: the moment of saying farewell to the house and countryside that had meant so much to him for so many years.

Adieu, dit-il,
Présence qui ne fut que pressentie
Bien que mystérieusement tant d'années si proche,

Adieu, image impénétrable qui nous leurra
D'être la vérité enfin presque dite,
Certitude, là où tout n'a été que doute, et bien que chimère
Parole si ardente que réelle.
Adieu, nous ne te verrons plus venir près de nous
Avec l'offrande du ciel et des feuilles sèches,
Nous ne te verrons pas rapprocher de l'âtre
Tout ton profil de servante divine.
Adieu, nous n'étions pas de même destin,
Tu as à prendre ce chemin et nous cet autre,
Et entre s'épaissit cette vallée
Que l'inconnu surplombe
Avec un cri rapide d'oiseau qui chasse.

           Farewell, he whispers,
Farewell, presence that was but dimly sensed,
Although for so many years so mysteriously close,
Farewell, unfathomable image that beguiled us
All the more as it was the truth almost spoken,
Certainty, when everything else was only doubt, and though
But a dream, speech so ardent it was real.
Farewell, no longer shall we see you come near us
With your offerings of sky and dry leaves,
No longer shall we see you bring toward the hearth
That profile of servant divine.
Farewell, our destinies were not the same,
You must take this path and we this other,
And between them grows deeper and denser
That valley which the unknown looms over
With the quick cry of the swooping bird of prey.

    The sense of leaving this place, of turning toward the un-
known, mingles with memories of other moments and other places
in the past, particularly those of early childhood. The poet manages
to translate the painful sense of loss into a confidence in the unfore-
seen, and to create from the strains of dispossession an autumnal
register that is as haunting as anything he has ever written. Like
all of Bonnefoy's work, this book is organized around the principle

of death and resurrection, disappointment and resurgent hope, farewell and new departure.

> *Et ils se disent que peu importe si la vigne*
> *En grandissant a dissipé le lieu*
> *Où fut rêvée jadis, et non sans cris*
> *D'allégresse, la plante qu'on appelle*
> *Bâtir, avoir un nom, naître, mourir.*

> *Car ils pressent leurs lèvres à la saveur,*
> *Ils savent qu'elle sourd même des ombres,*
> *Ils vont, ils sont aveugles comme Dieu*
> *Quand il prend dans ses mains le petit corps*
> *Criant, qui vient de naître, toute vie.*

> And they tell themselves that it hardly matters
> That the growing vines have scattered the place
> Where once, and not without cries of joy,
> They imagined the plant that people call
> Building, having a name, coming to birth, dying.

> For they press their lips to the savor of things,
> They know that it wells up even from the shadows,
> They go on, they are blind like God
> When he takes in his hands the tiny, crying
> Body that has just been born, all life.

∎ ∎ ∎

Shortly after the publication of *Ce qui fut sans lumière*, Bonnefoy was given the French Prix Goncourt for poetry and the *Hudson Review*'s Bennett Award. In 1991, he published a short book of verse called *Début et fin de la neige*, which pursues memories of a winter spent in Massachusetts and of walks in Hopkins Forest. The richly evocative meditations on the snow are always suggestive of the poet's fascination with the possibilities and limitations of the work he is doing with words.

> *Et parfois deux flocons*
> *Se rencontrent, s'unissent,*
> *Ou bien l'un se détourne, gracieusement*
> *Dans son peu de mort.*

D'où vient qu'il fasse clair
Dans quelques mots
Quand l'un n'est que la nuit,
L'autre, qu'un rêve?

And sometimes two flakes
Meet, unite,
Or else one turns away, gracefully,
Into its humble death.

How is it that daylight shines
In some words
When one is only night
The other, dream?

The snow focuses the poet's attention on a quintessentially ephemeral material, an always newly configuring substance. It thus speaks of the precarity of being and of the instability of every effort at inscription. But this is now a joyful recognition.

Flocons,
Bévues sans conséquences de la lumière.
L'une suit l'autre et d'autres encore, comme si
Comprendre ne comptait plus, rire davantage.

Snowflakes,
Harmless blunders of light.
One follows another, and still others,
As though understanding no longer mattered,
Only laughter.

■ ■ ■

While continuing to work on other poems in verse, Yves Bonnefoy has acknowledged a growing fascination with the possibilities of the prose poem. We thought it a good idea to include an example of this kind of writing—the recent *Là où retombe la flèche* (*Where the Arrow Falls*) (1988)—since it is a genre that Bonnefoy has practiced since the beginning of his career and since it promises to be a domain he will continue to explore. He has, in fact, spoken of the existence of a kind of "debate" in his present writing between verse and a poetic prose—freed "from the constraints of prosody"—, that would allow him to reestablish contact with "those other dimensions which had not been able to find their place in the music of the verse" and to "delve into their as yet unexplored depths."

· · ·

We end our collection with a charming meditation on the myth of Helen of Troy entitled "Wind and Smoke." It comes from a book called *La Vie errante* (*The Wandering Life*), published in 1993. The work is made up largely of poems in prose, but it also contains some poems in verse, including "Wind and Smoke." In this lyric, Bonnefoy gives moving expression to the convictions of a lifetime.

· · ·

Much of the emphasis in the French poetry inspired by Mallarmé has been on the idea of *absence:* the recognition of the fatal abolition of the signified by the signifier; the feeling that the "real life" is elsewhere and that society's use of language is a hopeless corruption; the conviction that the poet's mission is therefore to "give a purer meaning to the words of the tribe" and thus to establish, through a rarefied poetic speech, access to the true, to the ideal world compared to which the sorrowful place we languish in is an unfortunate impoverishment ruled by chaos and chance. Critics from Edmund Wilson to Jean-Paul Sartre have been quick to call into question the antisocial and world-denying implications of the Symbolist poetics. In his book *What Is Literature?*, Sartre, in fact, praises Bonnefoy himself for recognizing, even as a "young surrealist," what can become, for many artists, the fundamental difference between the exercise of words and the practice of living.

From the beginning, Bonnefoy's intuition of and insistence upon *presence* have set him apart. The emergence of presence in our experience of the world creates what the poet calls the "true place"; providing centrality, it invests the world with irrefutable significance and coherence, although at the moment they are lived these certainties have nothing to do with words. Indeed, words will never be able to recreate the reality of presence. What is hoped for from words, from the "few," from the "deep" words, is that they may be able to commemorate an experience of unity, of pleni-tude, and encourage the reader to rediscover his own such experi-ences, or to prepare him to meet them. It is the experience of presence that convinces Bonnefoy that it is in this world that the poet must work, and it is the knowledge that any aspect of this life may suddenly become the pathway to essential being that leads him to refuse the worlds proposed by words, and indeed by all modes of representation, since these may tend to become ends in themselves, and as such, forms of absence and excarnation.

Readers of Bonnefoy's work often raise three kinds of criticism of the way in which the idea of presence is offered. The first is that the affirmation of a world of presence is often presented in a highly abstract, "conceptual," and culturally mediated diction. The second is that Bonnefoy often does not so much recreate the reality of presence in his poems as simply designate, or even list, its manifes-tations in the life of the poet. The third criticism is that Bonnefoy does not give the reader enough intimate detail about his own personal experience, that the *specifically* human face is effaced or even obliterated in the highly "essentialized" landscape of his poetic world.

There can be no doubt that there is a profoundly paradoxical dimension to Bonnefoy's work. As a product of history who speaks of the importance of moments outside time, and as a speaker in a personal, idiosyncratic tongue that nonetheless establishes a sig-nificant dialogue with the language that a tradition has erected and embellished, Yves Bonnefoy has elaborated a poetic speech that places itself both inside and outside a long line of Western repre-sentation. But all great poetry, it could be argued, is born from just such a fundamental contradiction, and we might profitably read this poet's work from the perspective of how he confronts and seeks to come to terms with the contradictions that divide him. Clearly, the poet must at every moment both depart from the acquired and the known, thus venturing toward openness and renewal, and, at the same time, remain within a recognizable sys-tem of signs in order to communicate with others. If the poem were only the expression of what is initially experienced outside words, it would, presumably, be totally incomprehensible; if, on the other hand, it were only a description of this experience, it would become purely formulaic or conceptual, a kind of prose statement. Bonnefoy's poetry is neither of these things exclusively, and yet something of both worlds exists and may be discerned in it.

Two responses might be made to the charge—which was often leveled at T. S. Eliot as well—that, particularly in the later poetry, Bonnefoy tends to present the reader with an accumulation of lists, that he simply points to things, and that the evocation of presence is therefore insufficient: a kind of insistence rather than a rediscovery through words; an intellectual image which, through repetition, hardens into a verbal fetish. There is first of all, of course, Bonnefoy's own testimony that as his relation to language developed, as he attempted to "excavate" to the level of origins, to the place of absolute simplicity, he found those few, deep, elemental words that, in his view, are the "pillars upholding the vault of speech." Water, fire, earth, air, stone, tree: sacramental words that are like bread and wine. For Bonnefoy, these words are so fully steeped with what they name as to become for the poet who uses them, and lives them, more signified than signifier. Thus the poem strives to designate and retain only the "simple abundance" of the earth that all men share. And the poet therefore proposes "no longer to try to reabsorb what is in a formula, but, on the contrary, to reabsorb the formula in a participation in the real." Secondly, one might suggest that the "insufficiency" in the evocation of presence—the mere listing of things—is in part intentional, a deliberate effort to prevent the poem from becoming an end, a world, in itself. Shouldn't the reader *not* be absorbed in the glimpses of presence that the writing may vouchsafe, since these are only moments in a poem, and—Bonnefoy will never cease telling us this—the poem does not matter as much as life does? Doesn't he then deliberately send us away from the work and into our own life, giving us hints only, following—or leading us forth—with mere glimmers?

No human face in Yves Bonnefoy's world? It is certainly true that this poet tends to de-emphasize the particular differences that exist between people (and that are often explored by the artist who fusses over what he thinks sets him apart or makes him unique and superior) in favor of those experiences that are universal: birth, death, the experience of an elemental nature, of another person. His poetics aims at a pure ontology, through which words seek to elaborate a "common speech," so that "no longer being concerned with anything separated, closed off, they [words] dissipate the last enchantments of the mythical self, they speak of the simplest of human desires in the presence of the simplest of objects, which is being; they bring together the universal self." The many essays that Bonnefoy has written as homages to his friends—the pieces on Gaëton Picon, Paul Celan, Georges Seferis, Jean Starobinski, among many others—do, of course, bear witness to the importance in his life of those he has loved. But if friendship is clearly the arena for presence, it is also true that Yves Bonnefoy is the least sentimental of writers and one of the furthest removed from the cult of personality and from the fascination with individuality as such. And the poems, it seems to me, by expanding what is specific in personal experience, by disentangling the overdetermined understanding of it, by muting the aspects of a particular destiny, open their richness to what everyone has lived or felt: they sketch out the face and the hands that are everyman's.

■ ■ ■

Few poets ask to be read with a fuller commitment of one's own sense of wonder, and few will reward more completely the act of serious and patient adherence.

JOHN NAUGHTON

I

Du mouvement et de l'immobilité de Douve

▪ ▪ ▪

On the Motion and Immobility of Douve

1953
TRANSLATED BY GALWAY KINNELL

THÉÂTRE

I

Je te voyais courir sur des terrasses,
Je te voyais lutter contre le vent,
Le froid saignait sur tes lèvres.

Et je t'ai vue te rompre et jouir d'être morte ô plus belle
Que la foudre, quand elle tache les vitres blanches de ton sang.

II

L'été vieillissant te gerçait d'un plaisir monotone, nous méprisions
l'ivresse imparfaite de vivre.

«Plutôt le lierre, disais-tu, l'attachement du lierre aux pierres de
sa nuit: présence sans issue, visage sans racine.

«Dernière vitre heureuse que l'ongle solaire déchire, plutôt dans
la montagne ce village où mourir.

«Plutôt ce vent . . .»

III

Il s'agissait d'un vent plus fort que nos mémoires,
Stupeur des robes et cri des rocs—et tu passais devant ces flammes
La tête quadrillée les mains fendues et toute
En quête de la mort sur les tambours exultants de tes gestes.

C'était jour de tes seins
Et tu régnais enfin absente de ma tête.

THEATER

I

I saw you running on the terraces,
I saw you fight against the wind,
The coldness bled on your lips.

And I have seen you break and rejoice at being dead—O more
    beautiful
Than the lightning, when it stains the white windowpanes of
    your blood.

II

The dying summer had chapped you with listless pleasure,
we felt only scorn for the marred joys of living.

"Rather ivy," you would say, "the way it clings to the stones
of its night: presence without exit, face without roots.

"Last radiant windowpane ripped by the sun's claw, rather
in the mountains this village to die in.

"Rather this wind . . ."

III

It was a wind stronger than our memories,
Stupor of clothing and cry of rocks—and you moved in front of
    those flames,
Head graphlined, hands split open, all
Bent on death on the exulting drums of your gestures.

It was day of your breasts:
And you reigned at last absent from my head.

IV

Je me réveille, il pleut. Le vent te pénètre, Douve, lande résineuse endormie près de moi. Je suis sur une terrasse, dans un trou de la mort. De grands chiens de feuillages tremblent.

Le bras que tu soulèves, soudain, sur une porte, m'illumine à travers les âges. Village de braise, à chaque instant je te vois naître, Douve,

A chaque instant mourir.

V

Le bras que l'on soulève et le bras que l'on tourne
Ne sont d'un même instant que pour nos lourdes têtes,
Mais rejetés ces draps de verdure et de boue
Il ne reste qu'un feu du royaume de mort.

La jambe démeublée où le grand vent pénètre
Poussant devant lui des têtes de pluie
Ne vous éclairera qu'au seuil de ce royaume,
Gestes de Douve, gestes déjà plus lents, gestes noirs.

VI

Quelle pâleur te frappe, rivière souterraine, quelle artère en toi se rompt, où l'écho retentit de ta chute?

Ce bras que tu soulèves soudain s'ouvre, s'enflamme. Ton visage recule. Quelle brume croissante m'arrache ton regard? Lente falaise d'ombre, frontière de la mort.

Des bras muets t'accueillent, arbres d'une autre rive.

IV

I awaken, it is raining. The wind pierces you, Douve, resinous heath sleeping near me. I am on a terrace, in a pit of death. Great dogs of leaves tremble.

The arm you lift, suddenly, at a doorway, lights me across the ages. Village of embers, each instant I see you being born, Douve,

Each instant dying.

V

The arm lifted and the arm turned
Are simultaneous only for our dull wits,
But these sheets of greenness and mud thrown back,
What is left is a fire in death's kingdom.

The dismantled leg which the high wind pierces
Driving heads of rain before it
Will only light you to the threshold of that kingdom,
Douve's hands, hands already slower, dark hands.

VI

What paleness comes over you, underground river, what artery breaks in you, where your fall echoes?

This arm you lift suddenly opens, catches fire. Your face draws back. What thickening mist wrenches your eye from mine? Slow cliffs of shadow, frontier of death.

Mute arms reach for you, trees of another shore.

VII

Blessée confuse dans les feuilles,
Mais prise par le sang de pistes qui se perdent,
Complice encor du vivre.

Je t'ai vue ensablée au terme de ta lutte
Hésiter aux confins du silence et de l'eau,
Et la bouche souillée des dernières étoiles
Rompre d'un cri l'horreur de veiller dans ta nuit.

O dressant dans l'air dur soudain comme une roche
Un beau geste de houille.

VIII

La musique saugrenue commence dans les mains, dans les ge-
noux, puis c'est la tête qui craque, la musique s'affirme sous les
lèvres, sa certitude pénètre le versant souterrain du visage.

A présent se disloquent les menuiseries faciales. A présent l'on
procède à l'arrachement de la vue.

IX

Blanche sous un plafond d'insectes, mal éclairée, de profil
Et ta robe tachée du venin des lampes,
Je te découvre étendue,
Ta bouche plus haute qu'un fleuve se brisant au loin sur la terre.

Être défait que l'être invincible rassemble,
Présence ressaisie dans la torche du froid,
O guetteuse toujours je te découvre morte
Douve disant Phénix je veille dans ce froid.

VII

Wounded, lost among the leaves,
But gripped by the blood of vanishing paths,
Accomplice yet of life.

I have seen you, sunk down at struggle's end,
Falter at the edge of silence and water,
And mouth sullied by the last stars
Break with a cry the horrible nightwatch.

O raising into the air suddenly hard as rock
A bright gesture of coal.

VIII

The weird music starts in the hands, in the knees, then it is
the head that cracks, the music declares itself under the lips,
it surges across the underslope of the face.

Now the woodwork of the face comes apart. Now begins
the tearing out of the sight.

IX

White under a ceiling of insects, poorly lit, in profile,
Your dress stained by the venom of lamps,
I find you stretched out,
Your mouth higher than a river breaking far away on the
    earth.

Broken being the unconquerable being reassembles,
Presence seized again in the torch of cold,
O watcher always I find you dead,
Douve saying Phoenix I wake in this cold.

X

Je vois Douve étendue. Au plus haut de l'espace charnel je l'en-
tends bruire. Les princes-noirs hâtent leurs mandibules à travers
cet espace où les mains de Douve se développent, os défaits de leur
chair se muant en toile grise que l'araignée massive éclaire.

XI

Couverte de l'humus silencieux du monde,
Parcourue des rayons d'une araignée vivante,
Déjà soumise au devenir du sable
Et tout écartelée secrète connaissance.

Parée pour une fête dans le vide
Et les dents découvertes comme pour l'amour,

Fontaine de ma mort présente insoutenable.

XII

Je vois Douve étendue. Dans la ville écarlate de l'air, où com-
battent les branches sur son visage, où des racines trouvent leur
chemin dans son corps—elle rayonne une joie stridente d'insectes,
une musique affreuse.

Au pas noir de la terre, Douve ravagée, exultante, rejoint la
lampe noueuse des plateaux.

XIII

Ton visage ce soir éclairé par la terre,
Mais je vois tes yeux se corrompre
Et le mot visage n'a plus de sens.

La mer intérieure éclairée d'aigles tournants,
Ceci est une image.
Je te détiens froide à une profondeur où les images ne prennent plus.

X

I see Douve stretched out. On the highest level of fleshly space I hear her rustling. Black-princes hurry their mandibles across that space where Douve's hands unfold, unfleshed bones becoming a gray web which the huge spider lights.

XI

Covered by the world's silent humus,
Webbed through by a living spider's rays,
Already undergoing the life and death of sand
And splayed out secret knowledge.

Adorned for a festival in the void,
Teeth bared as if for love,

Fountain of my death living unbearable.

XII

I see Douve stretched out. In the scarlet city of air, where branches clash across her face, where roots find their way into her body—she radiates a strident insect joy, a frightful music.

With the black tread of earth, Douve, ravaged, exultant, returns to the highlands, this lamp.

XIII

Your face tonight lighted by the earth,
But I see your eyes' corruption
And the word face makes no sense.

The inner sea lighted by turning eagles,
This is an image.
I hold you cold at a depth where images will not take.

XIV

Je vois Douve étendue. Dans une pièce blanche, les yeux cernés de plâtre, bouche vertigineuse et les mains condamnées à l'herbe luxuriante qui l'envahit de toutes parts.

La porte s'ouvre. Un orchestre s'avance. Et des yeux à facettes, des thorax pelucheux, des têtes froides à becs, à mandibules, l'inondent.

XV

O douée d'un profil où s'acharne la terre,
Je te vois disparaître.

L'herbe nue sur tes lèvres et l'éclat du silex
Inventent ton dernier sourire,

Science profonde où se calcine
Le vieux bestiaire cérébral.

XVI

Demeure d'un feu sombre où convergent nos pentes! Sous ses voûtes je te vois luire, Douve immobile, prise dans le filet vertical de la mort.

Douve géniale, renversée: au pas des soleils dans l'espace funèbre, elle accède lentement aux étages inférieurs.

XVII

Le ravin pénètre dans la bouche maintenant,
Les cinq doigts se dispersent en hasards de forêt maintenant,
La tête première coule entre les herbes maintenant,
La gorge se farde de neige et de loups maintenant,
Les yeux ventent sur quels passagers de la mort et c'est nous dans
*   ce vent dans cette eau dans ce froid maintenant.*

XIV

I see Douve stretched out. In a white room, eyes circled with plaster, mouth towering, hands condemned to the lush grass entering her from all sides.

The door opens. An orchestra surges forward. And faceted eyes, woolly thoraxes, cold heads beaked and pincered, flood over her.

XV

O gifted with a profile where earth rages,
I see you disappear.

On your lips bare grass and flintsparks
Invent your last smile,

Deep knowledge which burns to ashes
The old bestiary of the mind.

XVI

Home of a dark fire where our slopes converge! Under its vaults I see you glimmer, Douve, motionless, caught in the vertical net of death.

Immaterial Douve, overturned: with the march of suns through funeral space, she reaches slowly the lower levels.

XVII

The ravine enters the mouth now,
The five fingers scatter in the forest now,
The primal head flows out among the grasses now,
The throat paints itself with snow and wolves now,
The eyes blow on which of death's passengers and it is we
    in this wind in this water in this cold now.

XVIII

*Présence exacte qu'aucune flamme désormais ne saurait restrein-
dre; convoyeuse du froid secret; vivante, de ce sang qui renaît et
s'accroît où se déchire le poème,*

*Il fallait qu'ainsi tu parusses aux limites sourdes, et d'un site
funèbre où ta lumière empire, que tu subisses l'épreuve.*

*O plus belle et la mort infuse dans ton rire! J'ose à présent te
rencontrer, je soutiens l'éclat de tes gestes.*

XIX

*Au premier jour du froid notre tête s'évade
Comme un prisonnier fuit dans l'ozone majeur,
Mais Douve d'un instant cette flèche retombe
Et brise sur le sol les palmes de sa tête.*

*Ainsi avions-nous cru réincarner nos gestes,
Mais la tête niée nous buvons une eau froide,
Et des liasses de mort pavoisent ton sourire,
Ouverture tentée dans l'épaisseur du monde.*

XVIII

Exact presence whom no flame can ever again hold back;
attendant of the secret cold; living, by that blood which
springs and flourishes there where the poem is torn,

It was necessary for you to appear, thus, at the numb limits,
to undergo this ordeal, this death-land where your light in-
creases.

O more beautiful, with death-steeped laughter! Now I dare
meet you, now I can face your gestures' flashing.

XIX

On the first day of cold the head escapes
As a prisoner flees into rarest air,
But Douve for an instant that arrow falls
And breaks its crown of palms on the ground.

So we had dreamed of incarnate gestures
But with mind cancelled we drink a cold water,
And death's banners flutter at your smile,
Attempted rift in the thickness of the world.

VRAI NOM

Je nommerai désert ce château que tu fus,
Nuit cette voix, absence ton visage,
Et quand tu tomberas dans la terre stérile
Je nommerai néant l'éclair qui t'a porté.

Mourir est un pays que tu aimais. Je viens
Mais éternellement par tes sombres chemins.
Je détruis ton désir, ta forme, ta mémoire,
Je suis ton ennemi qui n'aura de pitié.

Je te nommerai guerre et je prendrai
Sur toi les libertés de la guerre et j'aurai
Dans mes mains ton visage obscur et traversé,
Dans mon cœur ce pays qu'illumine l'orage.

■ ▫ ■

sans titre

La lumière profonde a besoin pour paraître
D'une terre rouée et craquante de nuit.
C'est d'un bois ténébreux que la flamme s'exalte.
Il faut à la parole même une matière,
Un inerte rivage au delà de tout chant.

Il te faudra franchir la mort pour que tu vives,
La plus pure présence est un sang répandu.

TRUE NAME

I will name wilderness the castle which you were,
Night your voice, absence your face,
And when you fall back into sterile earth
I will name nothingness the lightning which bore you.

Dying is a country which you loved. I approach
Along your dark ways, but eternally.
I destroy your desire, your form, your trace in me,
I am your enemy who shows no mercy.

I will name you war and I will take
With you the liberties of war, and I will have
In my hands your dark-crossed face,
In my heart this land which the storm lights.

■ ■ ■

untitled

If it is to appear, the deep light needs
A ravaged soil cracking with night.
It is from the dark wood that the flame will leap.
Speech itself needs such substance,
A lifeless shore beyond all singing.

You will have to go through death to live,
The purest presence is blood which is shed.

VRAI CORPS

Close la bouche et lavé le visage,
Purifié le corps, enseveli
Ce destin éclairant dans la terre du verbe,
Et le mariage le plus bas s'est accompli.

Tue cette voix qui criait à ma face
Que nous étions hagards et séparés,
Murés ces yeux: et je tiens Douve morte
Dans l'âpreté de soi avec moi refermée.

Et si grand soit le froid qui monte de ton être,
Si brûlant soit le gel de notre intimité,
Douve, je parle en toi; et je t'enserre
Dans l'acte de connaître et de nommer.

TRUE BODY

The mouth shut tight, the face washed,
The body purified, that shining fate
Buried in the earth of words,
And the most basic marriage is accomplished.

Silenced that voice which shouted to my face
That we were stranded and apart,
Walled up those eyes: and I hold Douve dead
In the rasping self locked with me again.

And however great the coldness rising from you,
However searing the ice of our embrace,
Douve, I do speak in you; and I clasp you
In the act of knowing and of naming.

DOUVE PARLE

I

Quelquefois, disais-tu, errante à l'aube
Sur des chemins noircis,
Je partageais l'hypnose de la pierre,
J'étais aveugle comme elle.
Or est venu ce vent par quoi mes comédies
Se sont élucidées en l'acte de mourir.

Je désirais l'été,
Un furieux été pour assécher mes larmes,
Or est venu ce froid qui grandit dans mes membres,
Et je fus éveillée et je souffris.

II

O fatale saison,
O terre la plus nue comme une lame!
Je désirais l'été,
Qui a rompu ce fer dans le vieux sang?

Vraiment je fus heureuse
A ce point de mourir.
Les yeux perdus, mes mains s'ouvrant à la souillure
D'une éternelle pluie.

Je criais, j'affrontais de ma face le vent . . .
Pourquoi haïr, pourquoi pleurer, j'étais vivante,
L'été profond, le jour me rassuraient.

DOUVE SPEAKS

I

Sometimes, you used to say, wandering at dawn
On blackened paths,
I shared the stone's hypnosis,
I was blind like it.
Now that wind has come by which all my games
Are given away in the act of dying.

I longed for summer,
A furious summer to dry my tears,
Now has come this coldness which swells in my flesh
And I was awakened and I suffered.

II

O fatal season,
O barest earth like a blade!
I longed for summer,
Who has broken off this sword in the old blood?

Truly I was happy
At this moment of dying.
Eyes lost, hands opening to the sullying
Of an eternal rain.

I cried out, I confronted the wind,
Why hate, why weep, I was alive,
The deep summer, the day reassured me.

III

Que le verbe s'éteigne
Sur cette face de l'être où nous sommes exposés,
Sur cette aridité que traverse
Le seul vent de finitude.

Que celui qui brûlait debout
Comme une vigne,
Que l'extrême chanteur roule de la crête
Illuminant
L'immense matière indicible.

Que le verbe s'éteigne
Dans cette pièce basse où tu me rejoins,
Que l'âtre du cri se resserre
Sur nos mots rougeoyants.

Que le froid par ma mort se lève et prenne un sens.

III

Let the word burn out
On this slope of being where we are stranded,
On this arid land
Which only the wind of our limits crosses.

Let him who burned standing up
Like a vine,
Let the wildest singer roll from the crest
Illuminating
Vast unutterable matter.

Let the word burn out
In this low room where you come to me,
Let the hearth of the cry close down
On our ember-words.

Let the cold by my death arise and take on meaning.

sans titre

Ainsi marcherons-nous sur les ruines d'un ciel immense,
Le site au loin s'accomplira
Comme un destin dans la vive lumière.

Le pays le plus beau longtemps cherché
S'étendra devant nous, terre des salamandres.

Regarde, diras-tu, cette pierre:
Elle porte la présence de la mort.
Lampe secrète c'est elle qui brûle sous nos gestes,
Ainsi marchons-nous éclairés.

■ ■ ■

sans titre

Qu'une place soit faite à celui qui approche,
Personnage ayant froid et privé de maison.

Personnage tenté par le bruit d'une lampe,
Par le seuil éclairé d'une seule maison.

Et s'il reste recru d'angoisse et de fatigue,
Qu'on redise pour lui les mots de guérison

Que faut-il à ce cœur qui n'était que silence,
Sinon des mots qui soient le signe et l'oraison,

Et comme un peu de feu soudain la nuit,
Et la table entrevue d'une pauvre maison?

untitled

So we will walk on the ruins of a vast sky,
The far-off landscape will bloom
Like a destiny in the vivid light.

The long-sought most beautiful country
Will lie before us land of salamanders.

Look, you will say, at this stone:
Death shines from it.
Secret lamp it is this that burns under our steps,
Thus we walk lighted.

■ ■ ■

untitled

Let a place be made for the one who approaches,
He who is cold and has no home.

He who is tempted by the sound of a lamp,
By the bright threshold of only this house.

And if he stays overcome with anguish and fatigue,
Let be uttered for him the healing words.

What needs this heart which was only silence,
But words which are both sign and litany,

And like a sudden bit of fire at night,
Or the table, glimpsed in a poor man's house?

LIEU DE LA SALAMANDRE

La salamandre surprise s'immobilise
Et feint la mort.
Tel est le premier pas de la conscience dans les pierres,
Le mythe le plus pur,
Un grand feu traversé, qui est esprit.

La salamandre était à mi-hauteur
Du mur, dans la clarté de nos fenêtres.
Son regard n'était qu'une pierre,
Mais je voyais son cœur battre éternel.

O ma complice et ma pensée, allégorie
De tout ce qui est pur,
Que j'aime qui resserre ainsi dans son silence
Le seule force de joie.

Que j'aime qui s'accorde aux astres par l'inerte
Masse de tout son corps,
Que j'aime qui attend l'heure de sa victoire,
Et qui retient son souffle et tient au sol.

PLACE OF THE SALAMANDER

The startled salamander freezes
And feigns death.
This is the first step of consciousness among the stones,
The purest myth,
A great fire passed through, which is spirit.

The salamander was halfway up
The wall, in the light from our windows.
Its gaze was merely a stone,
But I saw its heart beat eternal.

O my accomplice and my thought, allegory
Of all that is pure,
How I love that which clasps to its silence thus
The single force of joy.

How I love that which gives itself to the stars by the inert
Mass of its whole body,
How I love that which awaits the hour of its victory
And holds its breath and clings to the ground.

II

Hier régnant désert

■ ■ ■

Yesterday's Desert Dominion

1958
TRANSLATED BY ANTHONY RUDOLF

MENACES DU TÉMOIN

I

Que voulais-tu dresser sur cette table,
Sinon le double feu de notre mort?
J'ai eu peur, j'ai détruit dans ce monde la table
Rougeâtre et nue, où se déclare le vent mort.

Puis j'ai vielli. Dehors, vérité de parole
Et vérité de vent ont cessé leur combat.
Le feu s'est retiré, qui était mon église,
Je n'ai même plus peur, je ne dors pas.

II

Vois, déjà tous chemins que tu suivais se ferment,
Il ne t'est plus donné même ce répit
D'aller même perdu. Terre qui se dérobe
Est le bruit de tes pas qui ne progressent plus.

Pourquoi as-tu laissé les ronces recouvrir
Un haut silence où tu étais venu?
Le feu veille désert au jardin de mémoire
Et toi, ombre dans l'ombre, où es-tu, qui es-tu?

THREATS OF THE WITNESS

I

What did you want to set up on this table
If not the double fire of our death?
Frightened, I destroyed in this world
The red, bare table where the dead wind speaks.

Then I grew older. Outside, the truth of words
And the truth of wind have ceased their fight.
The fire has drawn away which was my church,
I am no longer even frightened. I do not sleep.

II

See, all the paths you went along are closed now,
No longer are you granted even the respite
To wander even lost. Earth, failing, sounds
With your footsteps which are going nowhere.

Why did you allow brambles to cover
That high silence you'd arrived at? The fire,
Empty, watches over memory's garden
And you, shadow in the shade, where are you, who are you?

III

Tu cesses de venir dans ce jardin,
Les chemins de souffrir et d'être seul s'effacent,
Les herbes signifient ton visage mort.

Il ne t'importe plus que soient cachés
Dans la pierre l'église obscure, dans les arbres
Le visage aveuglé d'un plus rouge soleil,

Il te suffit
De mourir longuement comme en sommeil,
Tu n'aimes même plus l'ombre que tu épouses.

IV

Tu es seul maintenant malgré ces étoiles,
Le centre est près de toi et loin de toi,
Tu as marché, tu peux marcher, plus rien ne change,
Toujours la même nuit qui ne s'achève pas.

Et vois, tu es déjà séparé de toi-même,
Toujours ce même cri, mais tu ne l'entends pas,
Es-tu celui qui meurt, toi qui n'as plus d'angoisse,
Es-tu même perdu, toi qui ne cherches pas?

V

Le vent se tait, seigneur de la plus vieille plainte,
Serai-je le dernier qui s'arme pour les morts?
Déjà le feu n'est plus que mémoire et que cendre
Et bruit d'aile fermée, bruit de visage mort.

Consens-tu de n'aimer que le fer d'une eau grise
Quand l'ange de ta nuit viendra clore le port
Et qu'il perdra dans l'eau immobile du port
Les dernières lueurs dans l'aile morte prises?

III

You no longer come into this garden,
The paths of suffering and aloneness vanish,
The grasses intimate your face of death.

It does not matter to you any more
That stone conceals the dark church, and that trees
Conceal the dazzled face of a redder sun,

For you it is enough
To take a long time dying as in sleep,
And now you do not even love
The shadow you will wed.

IV

Despite these stars you are alone now,
The center is far from you and near you,
You walked, you can walk, nothing changes now,
Always this same night which will never end.

See, you're separated from yourself now,
Always this same cry, but you do not hear it,
Are you dying, you who have no anguish now,
Are you even lost, you who seek after nothing?

V

The wind dies down, lord of the ancient sorrows,
Shall I be the last to take up arms for the dead?
Now the fire stirs only memory and ash,
Sound of a dead face, sound of a folded wing.

Do you consent to love only the iron of gray water
When the angel of your night closes the harbor
And loses in the still water of the harbor
Night's last glimmers caught in his dead wing?

Oh, souffre seulement de ma dure parole
Et pour toi je vaincrai le sommeil et la mort,
Pour toi j'appellerai dans l'arbre qui se brise
La flamme qui sera le navire et le port.

Pour toi j'élèverai le feu sans lieu ni heure,
Un vent cherchant le feu, les cimes du bois mort,
L'horizon d'une voix où les étoiles tombent
Et la lune mêlée au désordre des morts.

Only suffer through the harshness of my words
And I shall conquer sleep and death for you,
For you I'll summon in the breaking tree
The flame that will be both your ship and harbor.

And raise the fire which has no place, no time,
Wind seeking fire, the summits of dead wood,
The horizon of a voice where stars are falling,
Moon merging with the chaos of the dead.

LE PONT DE FER

Il y a sans doute toujours au bout d'une longue rue
Où je marchais enfant une mare d'huile,
Un rectangle de lourde mort sous le ciel noir.

Depuis la poésie
A séparé ses eaux des autres eaux,
Nulle beauté nulle couleur ne la retiennent,
Elle s'angoisse pour du fer et de la nuit.

Elle nourrit
Un long chagrin de rive morte, un pont de fer
Jeté vers l'autre rive encore plus nocturne
Est sa seule mémoire et son seul vrai amour.

IRON BRIDGE

No doubt there is still at the far end of a long street
Where I walked as a child a pool of oil,
Rectangle of heavy death under black sky.

Since then, poetry
Has kept its waters apart from other waters,
No beauty, no color can retain it—
Iron and night
Cause it to suffer.

It nourishes
A dead shore's long grief, an iron bridge
Thrown towards the other even darker shore
Is its only real love, its only memory.

LES GUETTEURS

I

Il y avait un couloir au fond du jardin,
Je rêvais que j'allais dans ce couloir,
La mort venait avec ses fleurs hautes flétries,
Je rêvais que je lui prenais ce bouquet noir.

Il y avait une étagère dans ma chambre,
J'entrais au soir,
Et je voyais deux femmes racornies
Crier debout sur le bois peint de noir.

Il y avait un escalier, et je rêvais
Qu'au milieu de la nuit un chien hurlait
Dans cet espace de nul chien, et je voyais
Un horrible chien blanc sortir de l'ombre.

II

J'attendais, j'avais peur, je la guettais,
Peut-être enfin une porte s'ouvrait
(Ainsi parfois dans la salle durait
Dans le plein jour une lampe allumée,
Je n'ai jamais aimé que cette rive).

Était-elle la mort, elle ressemblait
A un port vaste et vide, et je savais
Que dans ses yeux avides le passé
Et l'avenir toujours se détruiraient
Comme le sable et la mer sur la rive,

Et qu'en elle pourtant j'établirais
Le lieu triste d'un chant que je portais
Comme l'ombre et la boue dont je faisais
Des images d'absence quand venait
L'eau effacer l'amertume des rives.

THE WATCHERS

I

There was a passage at the far end of the garden.
I dreamed that I was walking down this passage.
Death approached with his tall withered flowers,
I dreamed I took the black bouquet from him.

In my bedroom were some shelves.
One evening I entered
And saw two shriveled women crying out
On the black painted wood.

There was a staircase and I dreamed
A dog howled in the middle of the night
In that space of no dog, and I saw
A dreadful white dog step out of the shadow.

II

Frightened, I waited. I watched out for him.
Perhaps at last a door did open
(Thus sometimes in broad daylight
A lamp kept burning in the room,
I have loved nothing but this shore).

Were it death it was indeed the image
Of a great empty harbor, and I knew
Past and future in his greedy eyes
Would continue to destroy each other
Like the sea and the sand on the shore,

And all the same I would create in him
The sad place of a song I bore
Like the mud and shadow I made into
Images of absence, when sea's water
Came to cleanse the shores of bitterness.

LA BEAUTÉ

Celle qui ruine l'être, la beauté,
Sera suppliciée, mise à la roue,
Déshonorée, dite coupable, faite sang
Et cri, et nuit, de toute joie dépossédée
—O déchirée sur toutes grilles d'avant l'aube,
O piétinée sur toute route et traversée,
Notre haut désespoir sera que tu vives,
Notre cœur que tu souffres, notre voix
De t'humilier parmi tes larmes, de te dire
La menteuse, la pourvoyeuse du ciel noir.
Notre désir pourtant étant ton corps infirme,
Notre pitié ce cœur menant à toute boue.

. . .

L'IMPERFECTION EST LA CIME

Il y avait qu'il fallait détruire et détruire et détruire,
Il y avait que le salut n'est qu'à ce prix.

Ruiner la face nue qui monte dans le marbre,
Marteler toute forme toute beauté.

Aimer la perfection parce qu'elle est le seuil,
Mais la nier sitôt connue, l'oublier morte,

L'imperfection est la cime.

BEAUTY

The one who ruins being—beauty—
Shall be tortured, broken on the wheel,
Dishonored, found guilty, made into cry
And blood, and night, of all joy dispossessed—
O you, torn apart on grates before the dawn,
O you, trampled on every road and pierced,
Our high despair shall be to see you live,
Our heart that you may suffer, and our voice
To humiliate you in your tears, to name you
Liar, procuress of the darkened sky,
Yet our desire being your frail body,
Our pity this heart that leads only to mire.

■ ■ ■

IMPERFECTION IS THE SUMMIT

There was this:
You had to destroy, destroy, destroy.
There was this:
Salvation is only found at such a price.

You had to
Ruin the naked face that rises in the marble,
Hammer at every beauty every form,

Love perfection because it is the threshold
But deny it once known, once dead forget it,

Imperfection is the summit.

À LA VOIX DE KATHLEEN FERRIER

Toute douceur toute ironie se rassemblaient
Pour un adieu de cristal et de brume,
Les coups profonds du fer faisaient presque silence,
La lumière du glaive s'était voilée.

Je célèbre la voix mêlée de couleur grise
Qui hésite aux lointains du chant qui s'est perdu
Comme si au delà de toute forme pure
Tremblât un autre chant et le seul absolu.

O lumière et néant de la lumière, ô larmes
Souriantes plus haut que l'angoisse ou l'espoir,
O cygne, lieu réel dans l'irréelle eau sombre,
O source, quand ce fut profondément le soir!

Il semble que tu connaisses les deux rives,
L'extrême joie et l'extrême douleur.
Là-bas, parmi ces roseaux gris dans la lumière,
Il semble que tu puises de l'éternel.

TO THE VOICE OF KATHLEEN FERRIER

All softness and irony assembled
For a farewell of crystal and haze.
The deep thrusts of the sword were near-silent,
The light of the blade was obscured.

I praise this voice mingled with gray,
Wavering in the distance of the song which died away
As if beyond pure forms there trembled
Another song, alone and absolute.

O light and light's nothingness, O you tears
Smiling higher than anguish or hope,
O swan, real place in unreal dark waters,
O wellspring in the very deep of evening!

It seems you know well the two shores:
The deepest sorrow and the highest joy.
Over there, in the light among the gray reeds
It seems that you draw from eternity.

sans titre

Aube, fille des larmes, rétablis
La chambre dans sa paix de chose grise
Et le cœur dans son ordre. Tant de nuit
Demandait à ce feu qu'il décline et s'achève,
Il nous faut bien veiller près du visage mort.
A peine a-t-il changé . . . Le navire des lampes
Entrera-t-il au port qu'il avait demandé,
Sur les tables d'ici la flamme faite cendre
Grandira-t-elle ailleurs dans une autre clarté?
Aube, soulève, prends le visage sans ombre,
Colore peu à peu le temps recommencé.

■ ■ ■

UNE VOIX

Écoute-moi revivre dans ces forêts
Sous les frondaisons de mémoire
Où je passe verte,
Sourire calciné d'anciennes plantes sur la terre,
Race charbonneuse du jour.

Écoute-moi revivre, je te conduis
Au jardin de présence,
L'abandonné au soir et que des ombres couvrent,
L'habitable pour toi dans le nouvel amour.

Hier régnant désert, j'étais feuille sauvage
Et libre de mourir,
Mais le temps mûrissait, plainte noire des combes,
La blessure de l'eau dans les pierres du jour.

untitled

Dawn, daughter of tears, restore
The room to its gray thing's peaceful state,
The heart to its good order. So much night
Required of this fire it wane and die.
We must keep vigil over the dead face.
It has hardly changed. . . . The ship of lamps,
Will it enter port as it required,
Turned to ashes on these tables, will the flame
Spread elsewhere into a different brightness?
Dawn, raise up, take the face without shadow,
Color bit by bit time's new beginning.

■　■　■

A VOICE

Hear me come to life again in these forests
Under the leaves of memory
Where green I pass by,
Burnt smile of ancient plants upon the earth,
Day's charry blood.

Hear me come to life again,
Lead you
Into the garden of presence,
Abandoned at evening, overcast by shadows,
Where, in this new love, you may find a dwelling.

Yesterday as desert reigned
I was wild leaf and free to die,
But time was ripening, black moan in the valleys,
The wound of water in the stones of day.

DELPHES DU SECOND JOUR

Ici l'inquiète voix consent d'aimer
La pierre simple,
Les dalles que le temps asservit et délivre,
L'olivier dont la force a goût de sèche pierre.

Le pas dans son vrai lieu. L'inquiète voix
Heureuse sous les roches du silence,
Et l'infini, l'indéfini répons
Des sonnailles, rivage ou mort. De nul effroi
Était ton gouffre clair, Delphes du second jour.

■　■　■

ICI, TOUJOURS ICI

Ici, dans le lieu clair. Ce n'est plus l'aube,
C'est déjà la journée aux dicibles désirs.
Des mirages d'un chant dans ton rêve il ne reste
Que ce scintillement de pierres à venir.

Ici, et jusqu'au soir. La rose d'ombres
Tournera sur les murs. La rose d'heures
Défleurira sans bruit. Les dalles claires
Mèneront à leur gré ces pas épris du jour.

Ici, toujours ici. Pierres sur pierres
Ont bâti le pays dit par le souvenir.
A peine si le bruit de fruits simples qui tombent
Enfièvre encore en toi le temps qui va guérir.

DELPHI, THE SECOND DAY

Here the unquiet voice agrees to love
Simple stone,
Flagstones time enslaves, delivers,
The olive tree whose strength tastes of dry stone.

The footstep in its true place. The unquiet
Voice happy beneath the rocks of silence,
And the infinite, the undefined response
Of death, shore, cattle bells. Your bright abyss
Inspired no awe, Delphi on the second day.

■ ■ ■

HERE, FOREVER HERE

Here, in the bright place. It is no longer dawn
But day, now, with its speakable desires.
Of a song's mirages in your dream, there is
Only this flashing of stones to come.

Here, until evening. The rose of shadows
Will turn upon the walls. The rose of hours
Will shed its petals without noise. The bright flagstones
Will lead as they please our steps in love with day.

Here, forever here. Stones upon stones
Have built the land spoken by memory.
Hardly does the sound of simple falling fruit
Fire time once more in you, time which will heal.

sans titre

La voix de ce qui détruit
Sonne encor dans l'arbre de pierre,
Le pas risqué sur la porte
Peut encore vaincre la nuit.

D'ou vient l'Oedipe qui passe?
Vois, pourtant, il a gagné.
Une sagesse immobile
Dès qu'il répond se dissipe.

Le Sphinx qui se tait demeure
Dans le sable de l'Idée.
Mais le Sphinx parle, et succombe.

Pourquoi des mots? Par confiance,
Et pour qu'un feu retraverse
La voix d'Oedipe sauvé.

untitled

The voice of what
Destroys still sounds
In the stone tree,
The step risked at
The door may yet
Conquer the night.

Whence Oedipus,
The one passing?
See, all the same,
He has prevailed.
Still wisdom fades
When he replies.

The Sphinx who keeps
Silent remains
In the sand of
The Idea.
But the Sphinx does
Speak, and succumbs.

Why words? Because
Of trust; and that
A fire may pass
Once again through
The voice of this
Oedipus, saved.

III

Pierre écrite

∎ ∎ ∎

Words in Stone

1965
TRANSLATED BY RICHARD PEVEAR AND EMILY GROSHOLZ

L'ÉTÉ DE NUIT

I

Il me semble, ce soir,
Que le ciel étoilé, s'élargissant,
Se rapproche de nous; et que la nuit,
Derrière tant de feux, est moins obscure.

Et le feuillage aussi brille sous le feuillage,
Le vert, et l'orangé des fruits mûrs, s'est accru,
Lampe d'un ange proche; un battement
De lumière cachée prend l'arbre universel.

Il me semble, ce soir,
Que nous sommes entrés dans le jardin, dont l'ange
A refermé les portes sans retour.

II

Navire d'un été,
Et toi comme à la proue, comme le temps s'achève,
Dépliant des étoffes peintes, parlant bas.

Dans ce rêve de mai,
L'éternité montait parmi les fruits de l'arbre
Et je t'offrais le fruit qui illimite l'arbre
Sans angoisse ni mort, d'un monde partagé.

Vaguent au loin les morts au désert de l'écume,
Il n'est plus de désert puisque tout est en nous
Et il n'est plus de mort puisque mes lèvres touchent
L'eau d'une ressemblance éparse sur la mer.

O suffisance de l'été, je t'avais pure
Comme l'eau qu'a changée l'étoile, comme un bruit
D'écume sous nos pas d'où la blancheur du sable
Remonte pour bénir nos corps inéclairés.

THE SUMMER'S NIGHT

I

It seems to me that the starry sky
Is swelling tonight, is drawing
Closer to us; and the dark,
Behind so many fires, is less obscure.

And the leaves, too, are shining under the leaves,
The green, and the orange of ripe fruit has deepened,
Lamp of a nearby angel; a flutter
Of hidden light runs through the universal tree.

It seems to me, tonight,
That we have come into the garden whose gates
The angel shut behind us forever.

II

The ship of one summer, and you
As if at the bow, in the fullness of time,
Unfolding painted cloths, talking softly.

In this May dream,
Eternity rose among the fruits of the tree,
And I offered you the fruit that unbinds the tree,
A shared world, with no anguish or death.

Far off the dead wander in the desert of foam,
No more a desert since all is within us
And no more death since my lips touch
The water of a likeness scattered on the sea.

O bounty of summer, I had you pure
As water changed by the star, as the sound
Of surf under our footsteps where the sand's whiteness
Shines back to bless our unlit bodies.

III

Le mouvement
Nous était apparu la faute, et nous allions
Dans l'immobilité comme sous le navire
Bouge et ne bouge pas le feuillage des morts.

Je te disais ma figure de proue
Heureuse, indifférente, qui conduit,
Les yeux à demi-clos, le navire de vivre
Et rêve comme il rêve, étant sa paix profonde,
Et s'arque sur l'étrave où bat l'antique amour.

Souriante, première, délavée,
A jamais le reflet d'une étoile immobile
Dans le geste mortel.
Aimée, dans le feuillage de la mer.

IV

Terre comme gréée,
Vois,
C'est ta figure de proue,
Tachée de rouge.

L'étoile, l'eau, le sommeil
Ont usé cette épaule nue
Qui a frémi puis se penche
A l'Orient où glace le cœur.

L'huile méditante a régné
Sur son corps aux ombres qui bougent,
Et pourtant elle ploie sa nuque
Comme on pèse l'âme des morts.

III

Movement
Had seemed a sin to us, so we went
Into stillness as the leaves of the dead
Stir and do not stir under the ship.

I called you my figure at the prow,
Happy, indifferent, who with half-closed eyes
Guide the ship of living
And dream as it dreams, being its deep peace,
Arched over the bow where love has always pulsed.

Smiling, wave-washed, primal,
Forever the shining of a motionless star
In the mortal gesture.
Beloved, in the long leaves of the sea.

IV

Earth as if rigged
For the wind,
This is the figure,
Red-stained, at your prow.

Star, water, and sleep
Have worn her bare shoulder
Which shivered and now turns
East where the heart freezes.

Meditative oil ruled
Her body in the moving shadows,
Yet she bends her neck
As souls of the dead are weighed.

V

Voici presque l'instant
Où il n'est plus de jour, plus de nuit, tant l'étoile
A grandi pour bénir ce corps brun, souriant,
Illimité, une eau qui sans chimère bouge.

Ces frêles mains terrestres dénoueront
Le nœud triste des rêves.
La clarté protégée reposera
Sur la table des eaux.

L'étoile aime l'écume, et brûlera
Dans cette robe grise.

. . . VI

Longtemps ce fut l'été. Une étoile immobile
Dominait les soleils tournants. L'été de nuit
Portait l'été de jour dans ses mains de lumière
Et nous nous parlions bas, en feuillage de nuit.

L'étoile indifférente; et l'étrave; et le clair
Chemin de l'une à l'autre en eaux et ciels tranquilles.
Tout ce qui est bougeait comme un vaisseau qui tourne
Et glisse, et ne sait plus son âme dans la nuit.

VII

N'avions-nous pas l'été à franchir, comme un large
Océan immobile, et moi simple, couché
Sur les yeux et la bouche et l'âme de l'étrave,
Aimant l'été, buvant tes yeux sans souvenirs,

N'étais-je pas le rêve aux prunelles absentes
Qui prend et ne prend pas, et ne veut retenir
De ta couleur d'été qu'un bleu d'une autre pierre
Pour un été plus grand, où rien ne peut finir?

V

It is nearly the hour
When day and night are no more, so great
Has the star grown to bless this brown body, smiling,
Limitless, water stirred by no chimera.

These fragile earthly hands will undo
The sad knot of dreams.
The shielded light will rest
On the table of the waters.

The star loves the foam,
And will burn in that gray dress.

. . . VI

For long it was summer. A motionless star
Overruled the turning suns. The summer's night
Bore the summer's day in its shining hands
And we talked together softly, in the leaves of night.

Indifferent star; ship's bow; and the bright path
From one to the other in quiet skies and seas.
Like a vessel turning, slipping, all that is
Moved, and no longer knew its soul in the night.

VII

Didn't we have summer to cross, like a wide
Still ocean, and I lying
On the eyes, the mouth, the soul of the ship's bow,
Loving summer, drinking your unmemoried eyes,

Wasn't I the vacant-eyed dream
That takes and does not take, and wants to keep
Of your summer color only a more intense blue,
Stone for a summer, where nothing would end?

VIII

Mais ton épaule se déchire dans les arbres,
Ciel étoilé, et ta bouche recherche
Les fleuves respirants de la terre pour vivre
Parmi nous ta soucieuse et désirante nuit.

O notre image encor,
Tu portes près du cœur une même blessure,
Une même lumière où bouge un même fer.

Divise-toi, qui es l'absence et ses marées.
Accueille-nous, qui avons goût de fruits qui tombent,
Mêle-nous sur tes plages vides dans l'écume
Avec les bois d'épave de la mort,

Arbre aux rameaux de nuit doubles, doubles toujours.

IX

Eaux du dormeur, arbre d'absence, heures sans rives,
Dans votre éternité une nuit va finir.
Comment nommerons-nous cet autre jour, mon âme,
Ce plus bas rougeoiement mêlé de sable noir?

Dans les eaux du dormeur les lumières se troublent.
Un langage se fait, qui partage le clair
Buissonnement d'étoiles dans l'écume.
Et c'est presque l'éveil, déjà le souvenir.

VIII

But your shoulder is torn among the trees,
Starry sky, and your mouth seeks
The breathing rivers of the earth to live
Through your anxious, yearning night among us.

O still our image,
You bear the same wound near your heart,
The same light where the same iron stirs.

Divide yourself, who are absence and its tides.
Receive us, who have the taste of fallen fruit.
Mingle us in the foam of your empty beaches
With the driftwood of death, tree

Of the doubling, the ever-doubling branches of night.

IX

Waters of the sleeper, tree of absence, shoreless hours,
In your eternity a night is ending.
How shall we name this new day, my soul,
This gentle glowing mixed with blacker sand?

In the waters of the sleeper the lights grow dim.
A language begins to form, which parts
The bright burgeoning of stars in the foam.
Awakening is near, and with it memory.

[R.P.]

L'ÉCUME, LE RÉCIF

Solitude à ne pas gravir, que de chemins!
Robe rouge, que d'heures proches sous les arbres!
Mais adieu, dans cette aube froide, mon eau pure,
Adieu malgré le cri, l'épaule, le sommeil.

Écoute, il ne faut plus ces mains qui se reprennent
Comme éternellement l'écume et le rocher,
Et même plus ces yeux qui se tournent vers l'ombre,
Aimant mieux le sommeil encore partagé.

Il ne faut plus tenter d'unir voix et prière,
Espoir et nuit, désirs de l'abîme et du port.
Vois, ce n'est pas Mozart qui lutte dans ton âme,
Mais le gong, contre l'arme informe de la mort.

Adieu, visage en mai.
Le bleu du ciel est morne aujourd'hui, ici.
Le glaive de l'indifférence de l'étoile
Blesse une fois de plus la terre du dormeur.

THE FOAM, THE REEF

Unscalable solitude, and so many paths!
Red dress, so many hours for us under the trees!
But farewell, in this cold dawn, my pure water,
Farewell despite the cry, the shoulder, the sleep.

Listen, we have no more need of these hands
That clutch each other as foam and rock do, eternally,
Nor even of these eyes that turn toward darkness,
Preferring sleep because it is still shared.

We must not keep trying to join voice and prayer,
Hope and night, longing for the deeps and the port.
You see, it is not Mozart fighting in your soul
But a gong, against the formless weapon of death.

Farewell, face in the light of May.
The blue sky is cheerless here, today.
Again the sword of the star's indifference
Wounds the sleeper's earth.

[R.P.]

sans titre

Bouche, tu auras bu
A la saveur obscure,
A une eau ensablée,
A l'Être sans retour.

Où vont se réunir
L'eau amère, l'eau douce,
Tu auras bu où brille
L'impartageable amour.

Mais ne t'angoisse pas,
O bouche qui demandes
Plus qu'un reflet troublé,
Plus qu'une ombre de jour:

L'âme se fait d'aimer
L'écume sans réponse.
La joie sauve la joie,
L'amour le non-amour.

untitled

Mouth, you will have drunk
Of the dark savor,
Of silted water,
Of Being without return.

Where the bitter water
Mingles with the sweet,
You will have drunk
Where unshareable love shines.

But do not be distressed,
O mouth that asks
For more than dim reflections,
More than shadows of day.

The soul is made by loving
The unresponding foam.
Joy gives life to joy,
Love saves what is not love.

[R.P.]

Prestige, disais-tu, de notre lampe et des feuillages,
Ces hôtes de nos soirs.
Ils tirent jusqu'à nous leurs barques sur les dalles,
Ils connaissent notre désir de l'éternel.

La nuit parfaite dans le ciel criant son feu,
Eux sont venus d'un pas sans ombre, ils nous éveillent,
Leur parole commence au tremblé de nos voix.

Le pas des astres mesurant le sol dallé de cette nuit,
Et eux mêlant à tant de feux l'obscurité propre de l'homme.

■ ■ ■

UNE PIERRE

Il désirait, sans connaître,
Il a péri, sans avoir.
Arbres, fumées,
Toutes lignes de vent et de déception
Furent son gîte.
Infiniment
Il n'a étreint que sa mort.

untitled

The spell, you said, of our lamp and the leaves,
These guests of our evenings.
They draw their boats up to us on the flags,
They know our thirst for the eternal.

While perfect night cries its fire overhead,
They come with shadowless steps and wake us,
Their speech begins at the tremor of our voices.

Stars pace out the paved ground of the night,
But they add a human darkness to so many fires.

[R.P.]

■ ■ ■

A STONE

He desired without knowing,
He died without having.
Trees, mists,
All lines of the wind and disappointment
Were his refuge.
He embraced
Nothing infinitely but his death.

[R.P.]

LE LIEU DES MORTS

Quel est le lieu des morts,
Ont-ils droit comme nous à des chemins,
Parlent-ils, plus réels étant leurs mots,
Sont-ils l'esprit des feuillages ou des feuillages plus hauts?

Phénix a-t-il construit pour eux un château,
Dressé pour eux une table?
Le cri de quelque oiseau dans le feu de quelque arbre
Est-il l'espace où ils se pressent tous?

Peut-être gisent-ils dans la feuille du lierre,
Leur parole défaite
Étant le port de la déchirure des feuilles, où la nuit vient.

THE PLACE OF THE DEAD

What is the place of the dead,
Do they have a right to move about as we do,
Do they speak, are their words more real,
Are they the spirit of the leaves, or higher leaves?

Has Phoenix built a castle for them
Or set them a table?
Is the call of a bird in the fire of a tree
The space they all crowd into?

Perhaps they rest in a leaf of ivy,
Their unmade speech
The port of the rent in the leaves, where night comes.

[R.P.]

UNE PIERRE

Je fus assez belle.
Il se peut qu'un jour comme celui-ci me ressemble
Mais la ronce l'emporte sur mon visage,
La pierre accable mon corps.

Approche-toi,
Servante verticale rayée de noir,
Et ton visage court.

Répands le lait ténébreux, qui exalte
Ma force simple.
Sois-moi fidèle,
Nourrice encor, mais d'immortalité.

A STONE

I was quite beautiful.
A day like this might resemble me.
But the thornbush triumphs over my face,
The stone weighs down my body.

Bend to me,
My vertical servant striped in black,
With your short face.

Pour out the shadowy milk that exalts
My simple strength.
Be faithful to me,
Still my nurse, but in immortality.

[R.P.]

UNE PIERRE

Ta jambe, nuit très dense,
Tes seins, liés,
Si noirs, ai-je perdu mes yeux,
Mes nerfs d'atroce vue
Dans cette obscurité plus âpre que la pierre,
O mon amour?

Au centre de la lumière, j'abolis
D'abord ma tête crevassée par le gaz,
Mon nom ensuite avec tous pays,
Mes mains seules droites persistent.

En tête du cortège je suis tombé
Sans dieu, sans voix audible, sans péché,
Bête trinitaire criante.

. . .

UNE PIERRE

Orages puis orages je ne fus
Qu'un chemin de la terre.
Mais les pluies apaisaient l'inapaisable terre,
Mourir a fait le lit de la nuit dans mon cœur.

A STONE

Your leg, deepest night,
Your breasts, bound,
So black, have I lost my eyes,
My nerves of agonized seeing
In this darkness harsher than stone,
O my love?

At the center of light, I abolish
First my head cracked by gas,
Then my name with all lands,
Only my straight hands persist.

At the head of the procession
I have fallen, godless, voiceless, sinless,
A crying trinitarian beast.

[R.P.]

■ ■ ■

A STONE

Storm after storm I was only
A path on the earth.
But the rains appeased the unappeasable earth,
Dying has made night's bed where my heart was.

[R.P.]

UNE VOIX

Nous vieillissions, lui le feuillage et moi la source,
Lui le peu de soleil et moi la profondeur,
Et lui la mort et moi la sagesse de vivre.

J'acceptais que le temps nous présentât dans l'ombre
Son visage de faune au rire non moqueur,
J'aimais que se levât le vent qui porte l'ombre

Et que mourir ne fût en obscure fontaine
Que troubler l'eau sans fond que le lierre buvait.
J'aimais, j'étais debout dans le songe éternel.

A VOICE

We grew old, he the leaves and I the pool,
He a patch of sunlight and I the depths,
He death and I the wisdom that chose life.

I consented that time would show us in the dark
His faun's face with its unmocking laugh,
I was glad that the dark-bearing wind would rise

And that dying was but a slight troubling
Of the fathomless water where the ivy drank.
I was glad, I stood in the eternal dream.

[R.P.]

LA CHAMBRE

Le miroir et le fleuve en crue, ce matin,
S'appelaient à travers la chambre, deux lumières
Se trouvent et s'unissent dans l'obscur
Des meubles de la chambre descellée.

Et nous étions deux pays de sommeil
Communiquant par leurs marches de pierre
Où se perdait l'eau non trouble d'un rêve,
Toujours se reformant, toujours brisé.

La main pure dormait près de la main soucieuse.
Un corps un peu parfois dans son rêve bougeait.
Et loin, sur l'eau plus noire d'une table,
La robe rouge éclairante dormait.

THE BEDROOM

The mirror and the river in flood, this morning,
Called to each other across the room, two lights
Appear and merge in the obscurity
Of furniture, within the unsealed room.

We were two realms of sleep, communicating
Through their courses of stone, where the untroubled
Water of a dream dispelled itself,
Forever recomposed, forever broken.

The pure hand slept beside the unquiet hand.
A body shifted slightly in its dream.
Far off, upon a table's blacker water,
Glittering, the red dress lay asleep.

[E.G.]

L'ARBRE, LA LAMPE

L'arbre vieillit dans l'arbre, c'est l'été.
L'oiseau franchit le chant de l'oiseau et s'évade.
Le rouge de la robe illumine et disperse
Loin, au ciel, le charroi de l'antique douleur.

O fragile pays,
Comme la flamme d'une lampe que l'on porte,
Proche étant le sommeil dans la sève du monde,
Simple le battement de l'âme partagée.

Toi aussi tu aimes l'instant où la lumière des lampes
Se décolore et rêve dans le jour.
Tu sais que c'est l'obscur de ton cœur qui guérit,
La barque qui rejoint le rivage et tombe.

THE TREE, THE LAMP

The tree grows older in the tree, it's summer.
The bird traverses birdsong and escapes.
The red dress gleams and in the sky disperses,
Far off, the burden of an ancient pain.

O fragile country,
Like the flame within a lamp one carries,
When sleep approaches, closed in the world's veins,
Simple the pulse in the soul that's shared.

You also love the moment when the light of lamps
Begins to fade and dream in day.
You know it is the darkness of your heart that heals,
The boat that gains the shore and falls.

[E.G.]

LE MYRTE

Parfois je te savais la terre, je buvais
Sur tes lèvres l'angoisse des fontaines
Quand elle sourd des pierres chaudes, et l'été
Dominait haut la pierre heureuse et le buveur.

Parfois je te disais de myrte et nous brûlions
L'arbre de tous tes gestes tout un jour.
C'étaient de grands feux brefs de lumière vestale,
Ainsi je t'inventais parmi tes cheveux clairs.

Tout un grand été nul avait séché nos rêves,
Rouillé nos voix, accru nos corps, défait nos fers.
Parfois le lit tournait comme une barque libre
Qui gagne lentement le plus haut de la mer.

MYRTLE

Sometimes I knew you as the earth, I drank
Upon your lips the anguish of springs
Welling among warm stones, and summer
Loomed above the rapt stone and the drinker.

Sometimes I called you myrtle and we burned
The tree of all your gestures all day long.
Those were the great brief fires of vestal light,
Thus I invented you in your bright hair.

A vast and empty summer scorched our dreams, rusted
Our voices, increased our bodies, broke our chains.
Sometimes the bed turned like a boat set free
That slowly gains the high, the open sea.

[E.G.]

LA LUMIÈRE DU SOIR

Le soir,
Ces oiseaux qui se parlent, indéfinis,
Qui se mordent, lumière.
La main qui a bougé sur le flanc désert.

Nous sommes immobiles depuis longtemps.
Nous parlons bas.
Et le temps reste autour de nous comme des flaques de couleur.

■ ■ ■

UNE VOIX

Combien simples, oh fûmes-nous, parmi ces branches,
Inexistants, allant du même pas,
Une ombre aimant une ombre, et l'espace des branches
Ne criant pas du poids d'ombres, ne bougeant pas.

Je t'avais converti aux sommeils sans alarmes,
Aux pas sans lendemains, aux jours sans devenir,
A l'effraie aux buissons quand la nuit claire tombe,
Tournant vers nous ses yeux de terre sans retour.

A mon silence; à mes angoisses sans tristesse
Où tu cherchais le goût du temps qui va mûrir.
A de grands chemins clos, où venait boire l'astre
Immobile d'aimer, de prendre et de mourir.

THE LIGHT OF EVENING

Evening,
These birds who talk together, indefinite,
Who peck and quarrel, light.
The hand that moves along the silent flank.

We have been motionless a long time now.
We're whispering.
And time lies round about like pools of color.

[E.G.]

■ ■ ■

A VOICE

How simple we were then, among those branches,
Not existing, walking side by side.
A shadow loving a shadow, and the space of branches
Silent under the weight of shadows, moveless.

I had turned you into a peaceful sleep,
Steps without tomorrows, days without becoming,
Nightowl in the bushes when pale evening falls,
Turning its eyes of earth upon us, irrevocable.

Into my silence, anguish without sadness
Where you sought the taste of ripening time.
Into great, closed roads, where the fixed star
Of loving, taking and dying came to drink.

[E.G.]

LA LUMIÈRE, CHANGÉE

Nous ne nous voyons plus dans la même lumière,
Nous n'avons plus les mêmes yeux, les mêmes mains.
L'arbre est plus proche et la voix des sources plus vive,
Nos pas sont plus profonds, parmi les morts.

Dieu qui n'es pas, pose ta main sur notre épaule,
Ébauche notre corps du poids de ton retour,
Achève de mêler à nos âmes ces astres,
Ces bois, ces cris d'oiseaux, ces ombres et ces jours.

Renonce-toi en nous comme un fruit se déchire,
Efface-nous en toi. Découvre-nous
Le sens mystérieux de ce qui n'est que simple
Et fût tombé sans feu dans des mots sans amour.

■ ■ ■

UNE PIERRE

Le jour au fond du jour sauvera-t-il
Le peu de mots que nous fûmes ensemble?
Pour moi, j'ai tant aimé ces jours confiants, je veille
Sur quelques mots éteints dans l'âtre de nos cœurs.

THE LIGHT, CHANGED

We see each other now in a different light,
Our eyes, our hands, will never be the same.
The tree is closer, sharper the voice of springs,
Our steps are deeper too, among the dead.

Touch us on the shoulder, absent god,
Cast our flesh in the weight of your return,
Finish mixing up our souls with stars,
With woods and birdsong, shadow-work and days.

Renounce yourself in us like tattered fruit,
Efface us in your hands. Somehow reveal
The hidden sense of mere simplicity,
Its fire gone, fallen on loveless words.

[E.G.]

■   ■   ■

A STONE

Day at the heart of day, can it redeem
The handful of words we used to be? For my part,
I loved those trusting days so much, I still keep watch
Over a few words, ash on our hearts' hearthstone.

[E.G.]

LA PAROLE DU SOIR

Le pays du début d'octobre n'avait fruit
Qui ne se déchirât dans l'herbe, et ses oiseaux
En venaient à des cris d'absence et de rocaille
Sur un haut flanc courbé qui se hâtait vers nous.

Ma parole du soir,
Comme un raisin d'arrière-automne tu as froid,
Mais le vin déjà brûle en ton âme et je trouve
Ma seule chaleur vraie dans tes mots fondateurs.

Le vaisseau d'un achèvement d'octobre, clair,
Peut venir. Nous saurons mêler ces deux lumières,
O mon vaisseau illuminé errant en mer,

Clarté de proche nuit et clarté de parole,
—Brume qui montera de toute chose vive
Et toi, mon rougeoiement de lampe dans la mort.

SPEECH AT EVENING

The land of early October had no fruit
That did not lie in tatters on the grass, its birds
Flew off with cries of absence and harsh losses
Along a high curved flank advancing towards us.

My speech at evening,
You are so cold, like grapes of some late autumn,
But wine already burns within your soul, and I can find
My only true warmth in your founding words.

The ship of bright October's swift conclusion
May come. And we can mix this pair of lights,
O my illuminated ship adrift at sea,

Brightness of night approaching, brightness of speech,
—Mist that will rise from every living thing
And you, my reddening lamp alight in death.

[E.G.]

LE LIVRE, POUR VIEILLIR

Étoiles transhumantes; et le berger
Voûté sur le bonheur terrestre; et tant de paix
Comme ce cri d'insecte, irrégulier,
Qu'un dieu pauvre façonne. Le silence
Est monté de ton livre vers ton cœur.
Un vent bouge sans bruit dans les bruits du monde.
Le temps sourit au loin, de cesser d'être.
Simples dans le verger sont les fruits mûrs.

Tu vieilliras
Et, te décolorant dans la couleur des arbres,
Faisant ombre plus lente sur le mur,
Étant, et d'âme enfin, la terre menacée,
Tu reprendras le livre à la page laissée,
Tu diras, C'étaient donc les derniers mots obscurs.

■ ■ ■

ART DE LA POÉSIE

Dragué fut le regard hors de cette nuit.
Immobilisées et séchées les mains.
On a réconcilié la fièvre. On a dit au cœur
D'être le cœur. Il y avait un démon dans ces veines
Qui s'est enfui en criant.
Il y avait dans la bouche une voix morne sanglante
Qui a été lavée et rappelée.

THE BOOK, FOR GROWING OLD

Stars moving from their summertime
To winter pastures; and the shepherd, arched
Over earthly happiness; and so much peace,
Like the cry of an insect, halt, irregular,
Shaped by an impoverished god. The silence
Rises from your book up to your heart.
A noiseless wind moves in the noisy world.
Time smiles in the distance, ceasing to be.
And in the grove the ripe fruit simply are.

You will grow old
And, fading into the color of the trees,
Making a slower shadow on the wall,
Becoming, as soul at last, the threatened earth,
You will take up the book again, at the still open page,
And say, These were indeed the last dark words.

[E.G.]

■ ■ ■

THE ART OF POETRY

The eyes were dragged up out of this night.
The hands immobilized and dried.
The fever reconciled. The heart has been told
To be the heart. The demon that lived in these veins
Has fled howling.
The dismal, blood-stained voice in this mouth
Has been washed and recalled.

[R.P.]

IV

Dans le leurre du seuil

■ ■ ■

In the Lure of the Threshold

1975
TRANSLATED BY JOHN NAUGHTON

LA TERRE

Je crie, Regarde,
La lumière
Vivait là, près de nous! Ici, sa provision
D'eau, encore transfigurée. Ici le bois
Dans la remise. Ici, les quelques fruits
A sécher dans les vibrations du ciel de l'aube.

Rien n'a changé,
Ce sont les mêmes lieux et les mêmes choses,
Presque les mêmes mots,
Mais, vois, en toi, en moi
L'indivis, l'invisible se rassemblent.

Et elle! n'est-ce pas
Elle qui sourit là («Moi la lumière,
Oui, je consens») dans la certitude du seuil,
Penchée, guidant les pas
D'on dirait un soleil enfant sur une eau obscure.

. . . .

Je crie, Regarde,
L'amandier
Se couvre brusquement de milliers de fleurs.
Ici
Le noueux, l'à jamais terrestre, le déchiré
Entre au port. Moi la nuit
Je consens. Moi l'amandier
J'entre paré dans la chambre nuptiale.

THE EARTH

I cry, Look,
The light
Was living there, so near us! Here, its store
Of water, still transfigured. Here the wood
In the shed. Here, the few fruits
Left to dry in the vibrations of the dawn sky.

Nothing has changed,
These are the same places and the same things,
Almost the same words,
But, look, in you, in me,
The undivided, the invisible are gathering.

And she! Is it not
She who is smiling there ("I the light,
Yes, I consent") in the certainty of the threshold,
Bending down, guiding the steps.
Of what seems a child-sun over dark waters.

. . . .

I cry, Look,
The almond tree
Is covered suddenly with thousands of flowers.
Here
The gnarled, the forever earthly, the torn,
Reach port. I the night
I consent. I the almond tree
I enter the bridal chamber, brightly adorned.

Et, vois, des mains
De plus haut dans le ciel
Prennent
Comme passe une ondée, dans chaque fleur,
La part impérissable de la vie.

Elles divisent l'amande
Avec paix. Elles touchent, elles prélèvent le germe.

Elles l'emportent, grainée déjà
D'autres mondes,
Dans l'à jamais de la fleur éphémère.

. . . .

O flamme
Qui consumant célèbres,
Cendre
Qui dispersant recueilles.

Flamme, oui, qui effaces
De la table sacrificielle de l'été
La fièvre, les sursauts
De la main crispée.
Flamme, pour que la pierre du ciel clair
Soit lavée de notre ombre, et que ce soit
Un dieu enfant qui joue
Dans l'âcreté de la sève.
Je me penche sur toi, je rassemble, à genoux,
Flamme qui vas,
L'impatience, l'ardeur, le deuil, la solitude
Dans ta fumée.
Je me penche sur toi, aube, je prends
Dans mes mains ton visage. Qu'il fait beau
Sur notre lit désert! Je sacrifie
Et tu es la résurrection de ce que je brûle.

And look, hands
From higher in the sky
Take,
Like passing rain, from every flower
The imperishable part of life.

They split open the kernel
Gently. They touch, they lift out the seeds.

They carry them off, beginnings already
Of other worlds,
In the forever of the ephemeral flower.

. . . .

O flame
That, destroying, consecrates,
Ash
That, scattering, brings together.

Yes, flame, that cleanses
From summer's sacrificial altar
The fevers, the writhings
Of clenched hands.
Flame, burning so that our shadow
May be washed from the stone of the clear sky
And so that a child god may frolic
In the bitterness of the sap.
I bend over you, passing flame.
Kneeling, I gather together
All the impatience, passion, solitude, and grief
And give them to your smoke.
I bend over you, dawn, I take
Your face in my hands. How beautiful the light
On our empty bed! I sacrifice
And you are the resurrection of what I burn.

Flamme
Notre chambre de l'autre année, mystérieuse
Comme la proue d'une barque qui passe.

Flamme le verre
Sur la table de la cuisine abandonnée,
A V.
Dans les gravats.

Flamme, de salle en salle,
Le plâtre,
Toute une indifférence, illuminée.

Flamme l'ampoule
Où manquait Dieu
Au-dessus de la porte de l'étable.
Flamme
La vigne de l'éclair, là-bas,
Dans le piétinement des bêtes qui rêvent.
Flamme la pierre
Où le couteau du rêve a tant œuvré.

Flamme,
Dans la paix de la flamme,
L'agneau du sacrifice gardé sauf.

. . . .

Et, tard, je crie
Des mots que le feu accepte.

Je crie, Regarde,
Ici a déposé un sel inconnu.

Flame
Our bedroom of the year before, full of mystery,
Like the prow of a passing ship.

Flame the glass
On the table in the deserted kitchen,
At V.
Amid the rubble.

Flame, from room to room,
The plaster,
Masses of indifference, made bright.

Flame the light bulb
Burning in the place above the stable door
Where God was missing.
Flame
The vine of lightning, over there,
Amid the hoofbeats of dreaming flocks.
Flame the stone
On which the knife of dream has labored so long.

Flame,
In the peace of the flame,
The sacrificial lamb kept safe.

. . . .

And, late, I cry out
Some words the fire accepts.

I cry, Look,
Here an unknown salt has settled.

Je crie, Regarde,
Ta conscience n'est pas en toi,
L'amont de ton regard
N'est pas en toi,
Ta souffrance n'est pas en toi, ta joie moins encore.

Je crie, Écoute,
Une musique a cessé.
Partout, dans ce qui est,
Le vent se lève et dénoue.
Aujourd'hui la distance entre les mailles
Existe plus que les mailles,
Nous jetons un filet qui ne retient pas.
Achever, ordonner,
Nous ne le savons plus.
Entre l'œil qui s'accroît et le mot plus vrai
Se déchire la taie de l'achevable.
O ratures, ô rouilles
Où la trace de l'eau, celle du sens
Se résorbant s'illimitent,
Dieu, paroi nue
Où l'érosion, l'entaille
Ont même aspect désert au flanc du monde.
Comme il est tard!
On voit un dieu pousser quelque chose comme
Une barque vers un rivage mais tout change.
Effondrements sur la route des hommes,
Piétinements, clameurs au bas du ciel.
Ici l'ailleurs étreint
La main œuvrante
—Mais quand elle dévie dans le trait obscur,
C'est comme une aube.

I cry, Look,
Your consciousness is not in you,
The source of your vision
Is not in you,
Your suffering is not in you, your joy even less.

I cry, Listen,
A music now has ceased.
Everywhere, in what is,
The wind rises up and unravels.
Today the space between the meshes
Is larger than the meshes,
We throw out a net that does not catch.
We no longer know how
To organize or finish.
Between the expanding eye and the truer word
The veil of the finishable is torn asunder.
O words crossed out, O gathering rust,
Where the traces of water, of meaning,
Grow limitless as they are reabsorbed,
God, bare wall
Where the erosion and the notches
Have the same deserted look on the flank of the world.
How late it is!
A god can be seen pushing something like
A barque toward a shore but then everything changes.
The roads of men have collapsed and are impassable,
There are hoofbeats, clamorings low in the sky.
Here the beyond clasps
The laboring hand
—But when it drifts into the darker line,
It is like a dawning.

Regarde,
Ici, sur la lande du sens,
A quelques mètres du sol,
C'est comme si le feu avait pris feu,
Et ce second brasier, dépossession,
Comme s'il prenait feu encore, dans les hauts
De l'étoffe de ce qui est, que le vent gonfle.
Regarde,
Le quatrième mur s'est descellé,
Entre lui et la pile du côté nord
Il y a place pour la ronce
Et les bêtes furtives de chaque nuit.
Le quatrième mur et le premier
Ont dérivé sur la chaîne,
Le sceau de la présence a éclaté
Sous la poussée rocheuse.
J'entre donc par la brèche au cri rapide.
Est-ce deux combattants qui ont lâché prise,
Deux amants qui retombent inapaisés?
Non, la lumière joue avec la lumière
Et le signe est la vie
Dans l'arbre de la transparence de ce qui est.

Je crie, Regarde,
Le signe est devenu le lieu.
Sous le porche de foudre
Fendu
Nous sommes et ne sommes pas.
Entre avec moi, obscure,
Accepte par la brèche au cri de faim.

Et soyons l'un pour l'autre comme la flamme
Quand elle se détache du flambeau,
La phrase de fumée un instant lisible
Avant de s'effacer dans l'air souverain.

. . . .

Look,
Here, on the barren stretches of meaning,
A few feet from the ground,
It is as though the fire had caught fire,
And this second bed of coals, dispossession,
It is as though it caught fire once more, at the heights
Of the stuff of what is, billowing in the wind.
Look,
The fourth wall has come unsealed,
Between it and the pile of stones on the north side
There is room for the brambles
And each night's furtive beasts.
The fourth wall and the first
Have shifted on the chain,
The seal of presence has burst
Beneath the rocky thrust.
And so I go in through the breach whose cry is brief.
Are these two fighters who have loosened their grip,
Two lovers who fall back unappeased?
No, the light plays with the light
And the sign is life
In the tree of the transparency of what is.

I cry, Look,
The sign has become the place.
Beneath the forked porch
Of lightning
We both are and are not.
Come in with me, dark,
Accept through the breach whose cry is hunger.

And let us be for one another like the flame
When it leaps from the torch,
A phrase of smoke, legible for a moment
Before vanishing into the sovereign air.

. . . .

Oui, toutes choses simples
Rétablies
Ici et là, sur leurs
Piliers de feu.

Vivre sans origine,
Oui, maintenant,
Passer, la main criblée
De lueurs vides.

Et tout attachement
Une fumée,
Mais vibrant clair, comme un
Airain qui sonne.

. . . .

Retrouvons-nous
Si haut que la lumière comme déborde
De la coupe de l'heure et du cri mêlés,
Un ruissellement clair, où rien ne reste
Que l'abondance comme telle, désignée.
Retrouvons-nous, prenons
A poignées notre pure présence nue
Sur le lit du matin et le lit du soir,
Partout où le temps creuse son ornière,
Partout où l'eau précieuse s'évapore,
Portons-nous l'un vers l'autre comme enfin
Chacun toutes les bêtes et les choses,
Tous les chemins déserts, toutes les pierres,
Tous les ruissellements, tous les métaux.

Yes, all simple things
Placed once more
Here and there, on their
Pillars of fire.

Yes, to live now
Without origin,
To pass by, hands riddled
With empty gleamings.

And every attachment
A band of smoke,
But ringing clear, like a
Trumpet that sounds.

. . . .

Let us find one another
So high that the light may seem to overflow
The cup of the hour and the cry mixed together,
A bright streaming, where nothing remains
But simple abundance, at last proclaimed.
Let us find one another, let us take up
By the handful our pure naked presence
On the bed of morning and the bed of evening,
Wherever time digs its ruts,
Wherever the precious water evaporates,
Let us go toward one another, as if we each
Had at last become every animal and every thing,
Every deserted road, every stone,
Every stream, every metal.

Regarde,
Ici fleurit le rien; et ses corolles,
Ses couleurs d'aube et de crépuscule, ses apports
De beauté mystérieuse au lieu terrestre
Et son vert sombre aussi, et le vent dans ses branches,
C'est l'or qui est en nous: or sans matière,
Or de ne pas durer, de ne pas avoir,
Or d'avoir consenti, unique flamme
Au flanc transfiguré de l'alambic.

Et tant vaut la journée qui va finir,
Si précieuse la qualité de cette lumière,
Si simple le cristal un peu jauni
De ces arbres, de ces chemins parmi des sources,
Et si satisfaisantes l'une pour l'autre
Nos voix, qui eurent soif de se trouver
Et ont erré côte à côte, longtemps
Interrompues, obscures,

Que tu peux nommer Dieu ce vase vide,
Dieu qui n'est pas, mais qui sauve le don,
Dieu sans regard mais dont les mains renouent,
Dieu nuée, Dieu enfant et à naître encore,
Dieu vaisseau pour l'antique douleur comprise,
Dieu voûte pour l'étoile incertaine du sel
Dans l'évaporation qui est la seule
Intelligence ici qui sache et prouve.

. . . .

Et nos mains se cherchant
Soient la pierre nue
Et la joie partagée
La brassée d'herbes

Look,
Here nothingness is flowering; but its petals,
Its colors of dawn and of twilight, its gifts
Of mysterious beauty to mortal earth,
And its dark green as well, and the wind in its branches,
This is the gold that is in us: immaterial gold,
Gold of not lasting, of not having,
Gold of having consented, only flame burning
On the transfigured flank of the alembic.

And so priceless the day about to end,
So precious the quality of its light,
So simple the slightly yellowing crystal
Of these trees, of these paths among the springs,
And so full of joy for one another
Our voices, which have longed to reunite
And which have wandered side by side, cut off,
Separated by darkness for so long,

That you might call this empty vase God,
God who is not, but who saves the gift,
Sightless God whose hands renew,
God a cloud, God a child and still to be born,
God the vessel for ancient sorrow understood at last,
God, arch for the faint star of the salt
In the evaporation which is the one
Intelligence here that knows and proves.

. . . .

And let our hands seeking one another
Be the naked stone,
And the joy we share,
An armful of grass

Car bien que toi, que moi
Criant ne sommes
Qu'un anneau de feu clair
Qu'un vent disperse

Si bien qu'on ne saura
Tôt dans le ciel
Si même eut lieu ce cri
Qui a fait naître,

Toutefois, se trouvant,
Nos mains consentent
D'autres éternités
Au désir encore.

. . . .

Et notre terre soit
L'inachevable
Lumière de la faux
Qui prend l'écume

Et non parce qu'est vraie
Sa seule foudre,
Bien que le vide, clair,
Soit notre couche

Et que toi près de moi,
Simples, n'y sommes
Que fumée rabattue
Du sacrifice,

For although both you and I,
Crying out, are
But a ring of bright fire
Scattered by the wind

So that soon,
In the sky, they will not know
If this cry that gave rise to birth
Even took place,

Still, finding one another,
Our hands consent
To other eternities
In desire once more.

. . . .

And let our earth be
The unending
Light of the scythe
That kindles the sea foam

And not because only
Its lightning is true,
Though the bright void
Be our bed,

Nor because you and I, simple,
Side by side there, are but
Smoke beaten back
Upon the sacrificial fire,

Mais pour sa retombée
Qui nous unit,
Blé de la transparence,
Au désir encore.

. . . .

Éternité du cri
De l'enfant qui semble
Naître de la douleur
Qui se fait lumière.

L'éternité descend
Dans la terre nue
Et soulève le sens
Comme une bêche.

. . . .

Et vois, l'enfant
Est là, dans l'amandier,
Debout
Comme plusieurs vaisseaux arrivant en rêve.

Il monte
Entre lune et soleil. Il essaie de pencher vers nous
Dans la fumée
Son feu, riant,
Où l'ange et le serpent ont même visage.
Il offre
Dans la touffe des mots, qui a fleuri,
Une seconde fois du fruit de l'arbre.

But for its falling
That makes us one,
Wheat of transparency,
In desire once more.

. . . .

Eternity of the cry
Of the child who seems
To be born of sorrow
Transformed into light.

Eternity comes down
Into the naked earth
And digs up meaning
The way a shovel might.

. . . .

And look, the child
Is there in the almond tree,
Standing upright,
Like a string of boats arriving in dream.

He climbs
Between moon and sun. He tries to bend toward us,
Through the smoke,
His laughing fire,
Where angel and serpent have the same face.
In the clusters of words that now have ripened,
He offers us
Once more from the fruit of the tree.

Et déjà le maçon
Se penche vers le fond de la lumière.
Sa bêche en prend les gravats
Pour le comblement impossible.

Il racle
De sa bêche phosphorescente
Cet autre ciel, il fouille
De son fer antérieur à notre rêve
Sous les ronces,
A l'étage du feu et de l'incréé.
Il arrache
La touffe blanche du feu
Au battement de l'incréé parmi les pierres.

Il se tait.
Le midi de ses quelques mots est encore loin
Dans la lumière.

Mais, tard,
Le rouge déteint du ciel
Lui suffira, pour l'éternité du retour
Dans les pierres, grossies
Par l'attraction des cimes encore claires.

. . . .

N'étant que la puissance du rien,
La bouche, la salive du rien,
Je crie,

Et au-dessus de la vallée de toi, de moi
Demeure le cri de joie dans sa forme pure.

. . . .

And the mason is already
Bending over the depths of the light.
His spade gathers up its rubble
For the impossible mending.

With his phosphorescent spade
He scrapes
At this other sky, digging
With the iron that came before our dream,
Beneath the brambles,
To the level of fire and the uncreated.
He tears up
The white tuft of fire
From the throbbing of the uncreated among the stones.

He says nothing.
The noonday of his few words is still far off
In the light.

But, late,
The faded red of the sky
Will be enough, for the eternity of his return
Among the stones, grown larger
From the attraction of hilltops still bright.

. . . .

Being but the power of nothingness,
The mouth, the saliva of nothingness,
I cry out,

And above the valley of you, and of me,
The cry of joy resides in its pure form.

. . . .

Oui, moi les pierres du soir, illuminées,
Je consens.

Oui, moi la flaque
Plus vaste que le ciel, l'enfant
Qui en remue la boue, l'iris
Aux reflets sans repos, sans souvenirs,
De l'eau, moi, je consens.

Et moi le feu, moi
La pupille du feu, dans la fumée
Des herbes et des siècles, je consens.

Moi la nuée
Je consens. Moi l'étoile du soir
Je consens.
Moi les grappes de mondes qui ont mûri,
Moi le départ
Des maçons attardés vers les villages,
Moi le bruit de la fourgonnette qui se perd,
Je consens. Moi le berger,
Je pousse la fatigue et l'espérance
Sous l'arche de l'étoile vers l'étable.
Moi la nuit d'août,
Je fais le lit des bêtes dans l'étable.
Moi le sommeil,
Je prends le rêve dans mes barques, je consens.

Et moi, la voix
Qui a tant désiré. Moi le maillet
Qui heurta, à coups sourds,
Le ciel, la terre noire. Moi le passeur,
Moi la barque de tout à travers tout,
Moi le soleil,
Je m'arrête au faîte du monde dans les pierres.

Yes, I the stones of evening, in the light,
I consent.

Yes, I the pool of water
Vaster than the sky, the child
Who stirs up its mud, the iris full of
The restless, memoryless reflections
Of the water, yes, I consent.

And I the fire, I
The pupil of the fire's eye, in the smoke
Of the grasses and the centuries, I consent.

I the cloud
I consent. I the evening star
I consent.
I the clusters of worlds that have ripened,
I the departure
Of the masons, going home late to their villages,
I the sound of their vans, fading in the distance,
I consent. I the shepherd,
I lead weariness and hope
Toward the stable beneath the bright arch of the star.
I the August night,
I make a bed for the animals in the stable.
I, sleep,
I take dream into my ships, I consent.

And I the voice
That desired so much. I the mallet
That struck the heavens, the black earth,
With muted blows. I the ferryman,
I the barque of all and through all,
I the sun,
I stop at the world's summit in the stones.

Parole
Décrucifiée. Chanvre de l'apparence
Enfin rouie.

Patience
Qui a voulu, et su.
Couronne
Qui a droit de brûler.

Perche
De chimères, de paix,
Qui trouve
Et touche doucement, dans le flux qui va,

A une épaule.

Speech
Uncrucified. Hemp of appearance
Retted at last.

Patience
That has wanted, and known.
Crown
That has the right to burn.

Pole
Of chimeras, of peace,
That finds
And gently touches, in the passing flow,

A shoulder.

L'ÉPARS, L'INDIVISIBLE
Extraits

Oui, par ce lieu
Perdu, non dégagé
Des ronces, puis des cendres d'un espoir.
Par ce désir vaincu, non, consumé

Car nous aurons vécu si profond les jours
Que nous a consentis cette lumière!
Il faisait beau toujours, beau à périr,
La campagne alentour était déserte,
Nous n'entendions que respirer la terre
Et grincer la chaîne du puits, cause du temps
Qui retombait du seau comme trop de ciel.
Nous travaillions ici ou là, dans de grandes salles,
Nous ne parlions que peu, à voix rouillée
Comme on cache une clef sous une pierre.
Parfois la nuit venait, du bout des longes,
Parfaite femme voûtée de noir poussant muettes
Ses bêtes dans les eaux du soleil constant.

Et qu'elle dorme
Dans l'absolu que nous avons été
Cette maison qui fut comme un ravin
Où bruit le ciel, où vient l'oiseau qui rêve
Boire la paix nocturne . . . Irrévélée,
Trop grande, trop mystérieuse pour nos pas,
Ne faisons qu'effleurer son épaule obscure,
Ne troublons pas celle qui puise d'un souffle égal
Aux réserves de songe de la terre.
Déposons simplement, la nuit venue, ces pierres
Où nous lisions le signe, à son flanc désert.

THE SCATTERED, THE INDIVISIBLE
Selections

Yes, by this place
Now lost, never fully freed
From the brambles, nor from the ashes of hope.
By this desire, vanquished, no, consumed

For we will have lived so fully the moments
That were granted to us by the light!
The days were beautiful, beautiful beyond our dreams,
The countryside around us was deserted,
We could only hear the breathing of the earth
And the creaking of the chain in the well, drawing up time
That spilled from the bucket like too much sky.
We would work here and there, in the vast rooms,
We spoke but little, in rusted voices,
As one might hide a key beneath a stone.
Sometimes night would come forward, from the end of the fields,
A perfect woman, dark, bending down, driving her silent
Beasts through the waters of the changeless sun.

And may it sleep
In the absolute that we have been,
That house which was like a ravine
Where the sky could rustle, where the dreaming bird
Could drink from night's peace . . . Unrevealed,
Too grand, too mysterious for our steps,
Let us but graze her dark shoulder,
Let us not trouble her, for she draws with even breath
From earth's store of dreams.
When night comes, let us simply place by her naked flank
These stones on which we seemed to read signs.

Que de tâches inachevables nous tentions,
Que de signes impénétrables nous touchions
De nos doigts ignorants et donc cruels!
Que d'errements et que de solitude!
La mémoire est lassée, certes, le temps étroit,
Le chemin infini encore . . . Mais le ciel
A des pierres plus rougeoyantes du côté
Du soir, et dans nos vies qui font étape,
Lumière qui t'accrois parfois, tu prends et brûles.

. . . .

Oui, par l'après-midi
Où tout est silencieux, étant sans fin,
Le temps dort dans la cendre du feu d'hier
Et la guêpe qui heurte à la vitre a cousu
Beaucoup déjà de la déchirure du monde.
Nous dormons, dans la salle d'en haut, mais nous allons
Aussi, et à jamais, parmi les pierres.

. . . .

Oui, par le corps
Dans la douceur qui est aveugle et ne veut rien
Mais parachève.

Et à ses vitres les feuillages sont plus proches
Dans des arbres plus clairs. Et reposent les fruits
Sous l'arche du miroir. Et le soleil
Est haut encore, derrière la corbeille
De l'été sur la table et des quelques fleurs.

. . . .

How many unfinishable tasks we tried,
How many unfathomable signs we touched
With fingers that knew nothing, and so were cruel!
How misguided we were, and how alone!
Memory is weary, certainly, and time narrow,
The journey still infinite . . . But the sky
Has stones that glow more brightly along the paths
Of evening, and at this stage our lives have reached,
Light that sometimes increases, you catch and burn.

. . . .

Yes, by the afternoon
When all is silent, being endless,
Time is sleeping in the ashes of yesterday's fire
And the wasp that knocks against the window has
Already sown up a great deal of the tear in the world.
We sleep, in the room upstairs, but we also
Walk, and forever, among the stones.

. . . .

Yes, by the body
In the gentle sweetness that is blind and wants nothing,
And yet brings completion.

And at its windows the leaves are closer
In brighter trees. And the fruit is at rest
Beneath the mirror's arch. And the sun
Is still high, behind the summer
Basket on the table and the handful of flowers.

. . . .

Oui, par naître qui fit
De rien la flamme,
Et confond apaisés
Nos deux visages.

(Nous nous penchions, et l'eau
Coulait rapide,
Mais nos mains, là brisées,
Prirent l'image.)

. . . .

Oui, par l'enfant

Et par ces quelques mots que j'ai sauvés
Pour une bouche enfante. «Vois, le serpent
Du fond de ce jardin ne quitte guère
L'ombre fade du buis. Tous ses désirs
Sont de silence et de sommeil parmi les pierres.
La douleur de nommer parmi les choses
Finira.» C'est déjà musique dans l'épaule,
Musique dans le bras qui la protège,
Parole sur des lèvres réconciliées.

. . . .

Oui, par les mots,
Quelques mots.

(Et d'une main,
Certes, lever le fouet, injurier le sens,
Précipiter
Tout le charroi d'images dans les pierres
—De l'autre, plus profonde, retenir.

Yes, by birth that made
A flame from nothing,
And mingles
Our two faces, now at peace.

(We bent down, and the water
Was flowing fast,
But our hands, though broken,
Caught the image.)

. . . .

Yes, by the child

And by these words I saved
For a child's mouth. "Look, the serpent
At the back of the garden hardly ever leaves
The lustreless shade of the boxtree. His only desire
Is for silence and for sleep among the stones.
The painfulness of naming among things
Will cease." There is already music in the shoulder,
Music in the arm that protects it,
Words on lips that have been reconciled.

. . . .

Yes, by words,
A few simple words.

(And with one hand,
Of course, raise the whip, curse meaning,
Drive
The whole load of images against the stones
—But with the other, deeper hand, rein back.

Car celui qui ne sait
Le droit d'un rêve simple qui demande
A relever le sens, à apaiser
Le visage sanglant, à colorer
La parole blessée d'une lumière,
Celui-là, serait-il
Presque un dieu à créer presque une terre,
Manque de compassion, n'accède pas
Au vrai, qui n'est qu'une confiance, ne sent pas
Dans son désir crispé sur sa différence
La dérive majeure de la nuée.
Il veut bâtir! Ne serait-ce, exténuée,
Qu'une trace de foudre, pour préserver
Dans l'orgueil le néant de quelque forme,
Et c'est rêver, cela encore, mais sans bonheur,
Sans avoir su atteindre à la terre brève.

Non, ne démembre pas
Mais délivre, et rassure. «Écrire», une violence
Mais pour la paix qui a saveur d'eau pure.
Que la beauté,
Car ce mot a un sens, malgré la mort,
Fasse œuvre de rassemblement de nos montagnes
Pour l'eau d'été, étroite,
Et l'appelle dans l'herbe,
Prenne la main de l'eau à travers les routes,
Conduise l'eau d'ici, minime, au fleuve clair.)

. . . .

For he who does not know
The right of a simple dream, that only asks
To raise up meaning, to soothe
The bleeding face, to color
The wounded word with light,
This man, be he
Almost a god, creating almost an earth,
Lacks compassion, does not attain to
The true, which is only a trusting, does not sense
In his desire clenched over his difference
The major drifting of the cloud.
He wants to build! Be it only a feeble
Trace of lightning, to preserve
In pride the emptiness of some form,
And this is dreaming too, but without joy,
Without having known how to reach the brief earth.

No, do not dismember
But deliver, and reassure. "Writing," a violence
But for the peace that tastes of pure water.
May beauty,
For this word has a meaning, in spite of death,
Do the work of bringing together our mountains
For the scant waters of summer
And call them into the grasses,
And take the water's hand across the roads
And lead the water here, the narrow water, to the bright river.)

. . . .

V

Ce qui fut sans lumière

■ ■ ■

In the Shadow's Light

1987

TRANSLATED BY JOHN NAUGHTON

L'ADIEU

Nous sommes revenus à notre origine.
Ce fut le lieu de l'évidence, mais déchirée.
Les fenêtres mêlaient trop de lumières,
Les escaliers gravissaient trop d'étoiles
Qui sont des arches qui s'effondrent, des gravats;
Le feu semblait brûler dans un autre monde.

Et maintenant des oiseaux volent de chambre en chambre,
Les volets sont tombés, le lit est couvert de pierres,
L'âtre plein de débris du ciel qui vont s'éteindre.
Là nous parlions, le soir, presque à voix basse
À cause des rumeurs des voûtes, là pourtant
Nous formions nos projets: mais une barque,
Chargée de pierres rouges, s'éloignait
Irrésistiblement d'une rive, et l'oubli
Posait déjà sa cendre sur les rêves
Que nous recommencions sans fin, peuplant d'images
Le feu qui a brûlé jusqu'au dernier jour.

Est-il vrai, mon amie,
Qu'il n'y a qu'un seul mot pour désigner
Dans la langue qu'on nomme la poésie
Le soleil du matin et celui du soir,
Un seul le cri de joie et le cri d'angoisse,
Un seul l'amont désert et les coups de haches,
Un seul le lit défait et le ciel d'orage,
Un seul l'enfant qui naît et le dieu mort?

THE FAREWELL

We have come back to our origin.
The place where all had been evident, now torn.
The windows mingled too many lights,
The stairs climbed too many stars
Which are collapsing arches, rubble;
The fire seemed to burn in another world.

And now birds fly from room to room,
The shutters have come down, the bed is covered with stones,
The fireplace full of the sky's dying debris.
It was here that we would talk at evening, almost in whispers,
Because of the echoing from the vaulted ceiling, here that
We would make our plans: but a boat,
Loaded with red stones, moved away,
Irresistibly, from a shore, and oblivion
Was already placing its ashes on the dreams
That we endlessly renewed, peopling with images
The fire that burned until the last morning.

Beloved, is it true
That in the language called poetry
There is only one word for designating
The morning and the evening sun,
One word for the cry of joy and the cry of anguish,
One for the woods upstream and the falling ax,
One for the unmade bed and the stormy sky,
One for the newborn child and the god who died?

Oui, je le crois, je veux le croire, mais quelles sont
Ces ombres qui emportent le miroir?
Et vois, la ronce prend parmi les pierres
Sur la voie d'herbe encore mal frayée
Où se portaient nos pas vers les jeunes arbres.
Il me semble aujourd'hui, ici, que la parole
Est cette auge à demi brisée, dont se répand
À chaque aube de pluie l'eau inutile.

L'herbe et dans l'herbe l'eau qui brille, comme un fleuve.
Tout est toujours à remailler du monde.
Le paradis est épars, je le sais,
C'est la tâche terrestre d'en reconnaître
Les fleurs disséminées dans l'herbe pauvre,
Mais l'ange a disparu, une lumière
Qui ne fut plus soudain que soleil couchant.

Et comme Adam et Ève nous marcherons
Une dernière fois dans le jardin.
Comme Adam le premier regret, comme Ève le premier
Courage nous voudrons et ne voudrons pas
Franchir la porte basse qui s'entrouvre
Là-bas, à l'autre bout des longes, colorée
Comme auguralement d'un dernier rayon.
L'avenir se prend-il dans l'origine
Comme le ciel consent à un miroir courbe,
Pourrons-nous recueillir de cette lumière
Qui a été le miracle d'ici
La semence dans nos mains sombres, pour d'autres flaques
Au secret d'autres champs «barrés de pierres»?

Certes, le lieu pour vaincre, pour nous vaincre, c'est ici
Dont nous partons, ce soir. Ici sans fin
Comme cette eau qui s'échappe de l'auge.

Yes, I think so, I want to think so, but who are
These shades that are carrying off the mirror?
And look, brambles are springing up among the stones
Along the barely beaten path through the grasses
That took us out toward the young trees.
It seems to me today, here, that speech
Is that half-broken trough flowing
At every rainy dawn with useless water.

The grass, and in the grass the water shimmering,
Like a river.
The work of mending in this world never ends.
Paradise lies scattered, this I know,
It is our earthly task to recognize
Its flowers that are strewn in the humble grass;
But the angel has disappeared, a light
That suddenly was but a setting sun.

And like Adam and Eve we will walk
One last time in the garden.
Like Adam the first regret, like Eve the first
Courage, we will want and not want
To pass through the low, half-opened door
Down there, at the other end of the field, colored
As though prophetically with a last ray of light.
Will the future spring from the origin
As the sky gives itself to a convex mirror?
From that light which has been the miracle
Of here and now, will we gather up
In darker hands the seeds for other pools of water
Hidden in other fields "among the stones"?

Surely the place of victory, of victory over ourselves,
Is here in what we are leaving tonight. Endlessly here
Like that water overflowing from the trough.

LE MIROIR COURBE

I

Regarde-les là-bas, à ce carrefour,
Qui semblent hésiter puis qui repartent.
L'enfant court devant eux, ils ont cueilli
En de grandes brassées pour les quelques vases
Ces fleurs d'à travers champs qui n'ont pas de nom.

Et l'ange est au-dessus, qui les observe
Enveloppé du vent de ses couleurs.
Un de ses bras est nu dans l'étoffe rouge,
On dirait qu'il tient un miroir, et que la terre
Se reflète dans l'eau de cette autre rive.

Et que désigne-t-il maintenant, du doigt
Qui pointe vers un lieu dans cette image?
Est-ce une autre maison ou un autre monde,
Est-ce même une porte, dans la lumière
Ici mêlée des choses et des signes?

II

Ils aiment rentrer tard, ainsi. Ils ne distinguent
Plus même le chemin parmi les pierres
D'où sourd encore une ombre d'ocre rouge.
Ils ont pourtant confiance. Près du seuil
L'herbe est facile et il n'est point de mort.

Et les voici maintenant sous des voûtes.
Il y fait noir dans la rumeur des feuilles
Sèches, que fait bouger sur le dallage
Le vent qui ne sait pas, de salle en salle,
Ce qui a nom et ce qui n'est que chose.

THE CONVEX MIRROR

I

Look at them down there, at that crossroads,
They seem to hesitate, then go on.
The child runs before them, they have picked
By the armful, for their few vases,
Those field flowers that have no name.

And the angel is above, watching them,
Enveloped in the wind of his colors.
One arm bare in the red cloth,
He seems to be holding a mirror, the earth
Reflected in the water of this other shore.

And what is he showing now with his finger
That is pointing toward a place in the image?
Is it some other house or some other world,
Is it even a door,
Among these things and signs now a single light?

II

They like to come in late like this. They cannot even
Make out the pathway that runs through the stones
Still welling with red and ochre shadow.
But they are not afraid. Near the doorway
The grass is easy and there is no death.

And here they are now beneath the vaulted ceilings.
It is pitch black and the dry leaves are stirring
On the flagstones, blown by the wind that never knows,
As it moves from room to room,
Which things have names and which are only things.

Ils vont, ils vont. Là-bas parmi les ruines,
C'est le pays où les rives sont calmes,
Les chemins immobiles. Dans les chambres
Ils placeront les fleurs, près du miroir
Qui peut-être consume, et peut-être sauve.

On, on they go. Down there among the ruins
Is the land where the shores are calm,
The paths motionless. They will put the flowers
In the rooms, near the mirror
That perhaps will consume and perhaps save.

PASSANT AUPRÈS DU FEU

Je passais près du feu dans la salle vide
Aux volets clos, aux lumières éteintes,

Et je vis qu'il brûlait encore, et qu'il était même
En cet instant à ce point d'équilibre
Entre les forces de la cendre, de la braise
Où la flamme va pouvoir être, à son désir,
Soit violente soit douce dans l'étreinte
De qui elle a séduit sur cette couche
Des herbes odorantes et du bois mort.
Lui, c'est cet angle de la branche que j'ai rentrée
Hier, dans la pluie d'été soudain si vive,
Il ressemble à un dieu de l'Inde qui regarde
Avec la gravité d'un premier amour
Celle qui veut de lui que l'enveloppe
La foudre qui précède l'univers.

Demain je remuerai
La flamme presque froide, et ce sera
Sans doute un jour d'été comme le ciel
En a pour tous les fleuves, ceux du monde
Et ceux, sombres, du sang. L'homme, la femme,
Quand savent-ils, à temps,
Que leur ardeur se noue ou se dénoue?
Quelle sagesse en eux peut pressentir
Dans une hésitation de la lumière
Que le cri de bonheur se fait cri d'angoisse?

Feu des matins,
Respiration de deux êtres qui dorment,
Le bras de l'un sur l'épaule de l'autre.

Et moi qui suis venu
Ouvrir la salle, accueillir la lumière,
Je m'arrête, je m'assieds là, je vous regarde,
Innocence des membres détendus,
Temps si riche de soi qu'il a cessé d'être.

PASSING BY THE FIRE

In the empty room, with its shutters closed,
And its lights spent, I passed by the fire.

And I saw that it still burned, that it was even,
At that moment, poised between
The powers of ash and of ember,
When the flame can choose to be
Either raging or subdued in the arms
Of what it has seduced on its bed
Of fragrant grasses and dead wood.
He is the jagged piece of branch I brought in
Yesterday, in the summer rain falling suddenly so hard.
He seems one of the gods of India, watching
With all the gravity of a first love
The one who asks of him that she be wrapped
In the lightning from before the worlds.

Tomorrow I will stir
The nearly cold flame, and doubtless
It will be a summer day like those
The sky offers to all the rivers, those of earth
And those, darker ones, of blood. Man and woman,
When do they ever know
That their passion is binding or coming apart?
What wisdom in their hearts could ever sense
That, as the light flickers,
Their cry of joy becomes a cry of anguish?

Morning fire,
The breathing of two people asleep,
The arm of one on the shoulder of the other.

And I who came
To open the room, let in the light,
I stop, I sit there, I watch you,
Innocence of the sprawling limbs,
Time so full it ceases to be.

DEDHAM, VU DE LANGHAM

I

Dedham, vu de Langham. L'été est sombre
Où des nuages se rassemblent. On pourrait croire
Que tout cela, haies, villages au loin,
Rivière, va finir. Que la terre n'est pas
Même l'éternité des bêtes, des arbres,
Et que ce son de cloches, qui a quitté
La tour de cette église, se dissipe,
Bruit simplement parmi les bruits terrestres,
Comme l'espoir que l'on a quelquefois
D'avoir perçu des signes sur des pierres
Tombe, dès qu'on voit mieux ces traits en désordre,
Ces taches, ces sursauts de la chose nue.

Mais tu as su mêler à ta couleur
Une sorte de sable qui du ciel
Accueille l'étincellement dans la matière.
Là où c'était le hasard qui parlait
Dans les éboulements, dans les nuées,
Tu as vaincu, d'un début de musique,
La forme qui se clôt dans toute vie.
Tu écoutes le bruit d'abeilles des choses claires,
Son gonflement parfois, cet absolu
Qui vibre dans le pré parmi les ombres,
Et tu le laisses vivre en toi, et tu t'allèges
De n'être plus ainsi hâte ni peur.

DEDHAM, SEEN FROM LANGHAM

I

Dedham, seen from Langham. The summer is somber,
Clouds are gathering. You might think that
The whole scene, the hedges, the distant villages,
The river, was about to vanish. That the earth
Was not even the eternity of the flocks and trees,
And that the chiming of bells, flung from
The church steeple, was also drifting away,
One more sound among the sounds of earth,
As the hope one sometimes has
Of having discovered signs written on stones
Falls when one examines more closely the tangle
Of markings: those shudders on the face of earth.

But you knew how to mix with your color
A kind of sand which welcomes
The glitterings of the sky in matter.
Where it was chance that spoke
Among the rubble, in the clouds,
You vanquished
With the beginnings of a music
The form which is the dead face of all life.
You listen to the sound of bees in the things filled with light,
To the way the buzzing sometimes seems to swell
Into that absolute in the meadow's shadows,
And you let it live in you, more transparent,
Since now you know neither haste nor fear.

Ô peintre,
Comme une main presse une grappe, main divine,
De toi dépend le vin; de toi, que la lumière
Ne soit pas cette griffe qui déchire
Toute forme, toute espérance, mais une joie
Dans les coupes même noircies du jour de fête.
Peintre de paysage, grâce à toi
Le ciel s'est arrêté au-dessus du monde
Comme l'ange au-dessus d'Agar quand elle allait,
Le cœur vide, dans le dédale de la pierre.

Et que de plénitude est dans le bruit,
Quand tu le veux, du ruisseau qui dans l'herbe
A recueilli le murmure des cloches,
Et que d'éternité se donne dans l'odeur
De la fleur la plus simple! C'est comme si
La terre voulait bien ce que l'esprit rêve.

Et la petite fille qui vient en rêve
Jouer dans la prairie de Langham, et regarde
Quelquefois ce Dedham au loin, et se demande
Si ce n'est pas là-bas qu'il faudrait vivre,
Cueille pour rien la fleur qu'elle respire
Puis la jette et l'oublie; mais ne se rident
Dans l'éternel été
Les eaux de cette vie ni de cette mort.

II

Peintre,
Dès que je t'ai connu je t'ai fait confiance,
Car tu as beau rêver tes yeux sont ouverts
Et risques-tu ta pensée dans l'image
Comme on trempe la main dans l'eau, tu prends le fruit
De la couleur, de la forme brisées,
Tu le poses réel parmi les choses dites.

O painter,
The wine is your gift,
Your hand, your divine hand,
As if pressing the grape; and thanks to you
The light is no longer that claw
That tears apart every form, every hope,
But rather joy, flowing in festive cups, however dark.
Thanks to you, landscape painter,
The sky has paused above the world
As did the angel above Hagar when she went,
With empty heart, into the labyrinths of stone.

And when you wish it so, how much fullness
Dwells within the murmur of the brook in the grass
As it gathers up the distant sounds of the church bells,
And how much eternity is offered in the scent
Of the simplest flower! It is as though earth
Consented gladly to what the spirit dreams of.

And the little girl who comes in dream
To play in the fields of Langham, and who
Sometimes looks toward Dedham in the distance, wondering
If it is not over there that one should live,
Picks, aimlessly, the flower she is smelling,
Then throws it aside and thinks no more
About it—but the waters of life,
Or death, are not rippled at all,
In the eternal summer.

II

Painter,
As soon as I knew you, I trusted you,
For even when you are dreaming, your eyes are open,
And should you risk your vision in images,
As one might plunge a hand into water, you always seize
The fruit of broken form, of broken color,
And you place it, real, among the names of things.

Peintre,
J'honore tes journées, qui ne sont rien
Que la tâche terrestre, délivrée
Des hâtes qui l'aveuglent. Rien que la route
Mais plus lente là-bas dans la poussière.
Rien que la cime
Des montagnes d'ici mais dégagée,
Un instant, de l'espace. Rien que le bleu
De l'eau prise du puits dans le vert de l'herbe
Mais pour la conjonction, la métamorphose
Et que monte la plante d'un autre monde,
Palmes, grappes de fruits serrées encore,
Dans l'accord de deux tons, notre unique vie.
Tu peins, il est cinq heures dans l'éternel
De la journée d'été. Et une flamme
Qui brûlait par le monde se détache
Des choses et des rêves, transmutée.
On dirait qu'il ne reste qu'une buée
Sur la paroi de verre.

Peintre,
L'étoile de tes tableaux est celle en plus
De l'infini qui peuple en vain les mondes.
Elle guide les choses vers leur vraie place,
Elle enveloppe là leur dos de lumière,
Plus tard,
Quand la main du dehors déchire l'image,
Tache de sang l'image,
Elle sait rassembler leur troupe craintive
Pour le piétinement de nuit, sur un sol nu.

Painter,
I give praise to your days, which are nothing more
Than the earthly task, delivered
From the haste that blinds it. Nothing more
Than the road, the slower road, up there
In the dust. Nothing more
Than the mountaintops of our world, but freed
For a moment from space. Nothing but the blue
Of the water drawn from the well in the green of the grass,
But for conjunction and metamorphosis,
And so that the plant of another world may spring up,
Palms, clusters of fruit still pressed close together,
In the resolution of the two colors, our sole life.
You paint, it is five o'clock in the eternity
Of the summer day. And a flame
That burned throughout the world breaks free
From things, from dreams, transmuted.
It seems that nothing remains but a faint cloud
Of mist on the surface of the alembic.

Painter,
The star in your landscapes is the one missing
In the infinite that crowds in vain the worlds.
It guides things toward their true places,
Then throws a cloak of light around their shoulders,
And later,
When the hand from the outside tears apart the image,
And splatters it with blood,
The star brings their frightened flocks together again
For the hoofbeats at night, against the naked earth.

Et quelquefois,
Dans le miroir brouillé de la dernière heure,
Elle sait dégager, dit-on, comme une main
Essuie la vitre où a brillé la pluie,
Quelques figures simples, quelques signes
Qui brillent au-delà des mots, indéchiffrables
Dans l'immobilité du souvenir.
Formes redessinées, recolorées
A l'horizon qui ferme le langage,
C'est comme si la foudre qui frappait
Suspendait, dans le même instant, presque éternel,
Son geste d'épée nue, et comme surprise
Redécouvrait le pays de l'enfance,
Parcourant ses chemins; et, pensive, touchait
Les objets oubliés, les vêtements
Dans de vieilles armoires, les deux ou trois
Jouets mystérieux de sa première
Allégresse divine. Elle, la mort,
Elle défait le temps qui va le monde,
Montre le mur qu'éclaire le couchant,
Et mène autour de la maison vers la tonnelle
Pour offrir, ô bonheur ici, dans l'heure brève,
Les fruits, les voix, les reflets, les rumeurs,
Le vin léger dans rien que la lumière.

And sometimes,
In the blurred mirror of the last hour,
They say that the star knows how to draw forth,
As a hand wipes a window pane that shone with rain,
A few simple figures, a few signs
Gleaming beyond words, indecipherable
In the motionlessness of memory,
Forms that are drawn and colored anew
On the horizon that closes our language;
It is as though the lightning, as it struck,
Held back its naked sword, and with surprise,
At that very instant, almost eternal,
Rediscovered the land of childhood,
Wandered along its paths; and touched once more,
With pensive hands, things long forgotten; the clothes
That languish in old closets, the two or three
Mysterious toys from the child's first moments
Of joyfulness divine. This light, this death
Undoes time as it roams throughout the world;
Shows us the wall all lit up at sunset
And leads us around the house and toward the arbor
To offer, for one brief moment, O blissfulness,
The fruit, the voices, the shadows, the sounds,
The gentle wine, in nothing but the light.

LA BARQUE AUX DEUX SOMMEILS

I

Glisse la barque étroite aux deux sommeils
Qui respirent l'un près de l'autre, sans recherche
De rien, dans l'immobilité, qu'un même souffle.
À l'aube le courant va plus rapide,
La barre qu'on n'entend pas de nuit gronde là-bas,
L'enfant qui joue à l'avant de la barque

Alors a compassion et se rapproche
Car ceux qui dorment là n'ont pas de visage,
Rien que ces deux flancs nus qui firent confiance
L'un à la joie de l'autre; et l'aube est froide,
L'eau sombre a des reflets d'une autre lumière.

Il s'approche, il se penche,
Il voit dans leur travail l'homme, la femme,
C'est une terre pauvre, dont les voies
Sont emplies d'eau comme après les orages.
Il place dans ce sol
Le germe d'une plante, qui recouvre
De ses palmes bientôt, sans souvenirs,
Le lieu de l'origine, aux rives basses.
C'est elle qu'il pressent, depuis déjà
Les premiers mots en lui, quand il regarde
Monter le soir ces piliers de fumée
Là-bas, loin dans la paix des deux branches du fleuve.

Et c'est elle qu'il veut, contre le ciel,
Voir croître chaque jour, dans l'évidence
Des oiseaux qui se croisent en criant.
Il ira tard le soir dans son feuillage,
Il cherchera le fruit dans la couleur,
Il en pressera l'or dans ses mains paisibles,

THE BOAT OF THE TWO DREAMS

Over the waters glides the narrow boat, two dreamers
Breathing beside one another; they seek,
In the stillness, nothing but to be the same breath.
At dawn, the current flows more swiftly,
The shoal, which is inaudible at night,
Can now be heard grumbling somewhere down there,
The child playing at the prow of the boat

Takes pity then and comes closer,
For those sleeping near him are faceless,
Being only these two bare flanks that trusted
In each other's joy; and dawn is cold,
The dark water reflects another sky.

He draws near and bends down,
He sees the man, the woman, in the midst of their labor,
It is but a poor earth, whose paths
Are filled with water, as after storms.
He places in this ground
The seed of a plant that soon
Covers with its palms, memoryless,
The low-banked place where all things began.
He had sensed it, ever since
The very first words in him, as he watched
Those pillars of smoke rising at evening,
Down there, far off in the peacefulness
Of the two long branches of the river.

And now, it is what he wants to see growing
Each day against the sky in the bright clearness
Of the birds that cross each other, clamoring.
Late at evening, he will go among its leaves,
There he will seek the fruit in the color,
He will press its pure gold in his quiet hands,

Puis il prendra la barque, il ira poser
Le vin du temps désert, dans une jarre,
Au pied du dieu du rêve, agenouillé
Les yeux clos, souriant,
Dans les herbes lourdes de graines du bord du fleuve.

II

Ils dorment. Fut vaincu enfin le temps qui œuvre
Contre toute confiance, toute joie.
Peut-être même que leur forme laisse sourdre
La lumière du rêve, qui ruisselle
Devant beaucoup des barques qui avancent
Avant le jour dans les pays de palmes.

Ils dorment. Et l'enfant revient à la proue,
Il contemple à nouveau, qui étincelle
Maintenant, l'eau du fleuve. Puis il rassemble
Des branches pour le feu, qu'il allume, serré
Dans un vase de terre. Et il s'endort,
Coloré par la flamme qui veille seule.

III

Ils rêvent. Dans la vie comme dans les images
C'est vrai que la valeur la plus claire avoisine
L'ombre noire de là où les mots se nouent
Dans la gorge de ceux qui ne savent dire
Pourquoi ils cherchent tant, dans le temps désert.

Ils vont. Et la couleur qui brasse la nuée
Prend parfois par hasard dans ses mains de sable
Leur désir le plus nu, leur guerre, leur regret
Le plus cruel, pour en faire l'immense
Château illuminé d'une autre rive.

Then he will take the boat, and he will go
To place this wine of empty Time, in a jar,
At the foot of the god of dreams, who kneels,
Smiling, his eyes closed,
In the seed-swollen grasses of the river bank.

II

They are sleeping. Time, that works against
All confidence, and joy, has been vanquished.
Who knows? Perhaps their form allows the light
Of their dream to well up, this light that flows
Before so many of the boats that move
Forward, at break of day, in the land of palms.

They are sleeping. And the child returns to the prow,
Once again he looks at the river water,
Which is glistening now. Then he gathers
Branches for the fire, which he lights, packed
In an earthen vessel. And he goes to sleep,
Lit up by the flame that stands watch alone.

III

They dream. In life, as in images,
The brightest spot is near the darker shadow,
Which is the place in words where words knot up
In the throats of those who can never say
Why they are searching so, in the deserts of time.

They go. And the color that stirs the cloud
Sometimes happens to take in its hands of sand
Their most naked desire, their war, their cruelest
Regret, to make of them the vast,
Illuminated castle of another shore.

IV

L'étoile dans la chose a reparu,
Elle en grossit le grain qui se fait moins trouble,
La grappe de ce qui est donne à nouveau
La joie simple de boire à ceux qui errent,
Les yeux emplis de quelque souvenir.

Et ils se disent que peu importe si la vigne
En grandissant a dissipé le lieu
Où fut rêvée jadis, et non sans cris
D'allégresse, la plante qu'on appelle
Bâtir, avoir un nom, naître, mourir.

Car ils pressent leurs lèvres à la saveur,
Ils savent qu'elle sourd même des ombres,
Ils vont, ils sont aveugles comme Dieu
Quand il prend dans ses mains le petit corps
Criant, qui vient de naître, toute vie.

Et tout alors, c'est comme un vase qui prend forme,
La couleur et le sable se sont unis.
Les mondes de l'imaginaire se dissipent.
Quelque chose s'ébauche qui ressemble
À des cailloux qui brillent dans l'eau claire.

IV

The star in things has reappeared,
It swells their grain which is less obscure,
The clusters of what is give once again
The simple joy of drinking to those who wander,
Their eyes filled with some memory.

And they tell themselves that it hardly matters
That the growing vines have scattered the place
Where once, and not without cries of joy,
They imagined the plant that people call
Building, having a name, coming to birth, dying.

For they press their lips to the savor of things,
They know that it wells up even from the shadows,
They go on, they are blind like God
When he takes in his hands the tiny, crying
Body that has just been born, all life.

And everything then is like a vase as it takes shape,
Color and sand are joined together.
The imaginary worlds are dispelled.
The outline of something takes form
That is like pebbles gleaming in clear water.

VI

Là où retombe la flèche

■ ■ ■

Where the Arrow Falls

1988
TRANSLATED BY RICHARD STAMELMAN

Perdu. A quelques pas de la maison, cependant, à guère plus que trois jets de pierre.

Là où retombe la flèche qui fut lancée au hasard.

Perdu, sans drame. On me retrouvera. Des voix se dresseront de toutes parts sur le ciel, dans la nuit qui tombe.

Et il n'est que quatre heures, il y a donc encore beaucoup de jour pour continuer à se perdre—allant, courant parfois, revenant— parmi ces pierres brisées et ces chênes gris dans le bois coupé de ravins qui cherche partout l'infini, sous l'horizon tumultueux, mais ici, devant le pas, se resserre.

Nécessairement, je vais rencontrer une route.

Je verrai une grange en ruine, d'où partait bien une piste.

Appellerai-je? Non, pas encore.

Perdu, pourtant. Car il lui faut décider, presque à tout instant, et voici qu'il ne peut le faire. Rien ne lui parle, rien ne lui est plus un indice. L'idée même d'indice se dissipe. Dans l'empreinte qu'avait laissée la parole, sur ce qui est, l'eau de l'apparence déserte est remontée, brille seule.

Chaque mot: quelque chose de clos maintenant, une surface mate sans rien qui vibre, une pierre.

Il peut l'articuler, il peut dire: le chêne. Mais quand il a dit: le chêne—et à voix haute, pourquoi?—le mot reste, dans son esprit, comme dans la main la clef qui n'a pas joué se fait lourde. Et la figure de l'arbre se clive, se fragmente, et se rassemble plus haut, dans l'absolu, comme quand on regarde ces bossellements du verre qu'il y a dans d'anciennes vitres.

La couleur, rejetée sur le bord de l'image par le gonflement dans le verre. Ce qu'on appelle la forme troué d'un ressaut—démenti. Comme si s'était ouverte la main qui garde serrées couleurs et formes.

Lost. Only a few steps, however, from the house, no more than three times a stone's throw.

There where the arrow haphazardly falls.

Lost, merely lost. They will find me. Voices from all parts will appear under the sky, in the falling night.

It is only four o'clock; so there is still plenty of light to keep losing one's way—moving, running, from time to time, turning back—among these broken stones and gray oaks in the ravine-cut woods that, beneath the stormy horizon, seek the infinite, although here they close in around my steps.

Surely, I will come upon a road.

I will see a barn in ruins where a trail once began.

Shall I call out? No, not yet.

And yet, lost. At almost every moment he must decide what to do, and yet he cannot. Nothing speaks to him, nothing is a sign any longer. Even the notion of a sign vanishes. Within the trace left by the word on what exists, the water of meaningless appearance rises up, shines alone.

Each word is something impenetrable now; a dull surface where nothing stirs, a stone.

He can articulate it; he can say "oak tree." But when these words have been spoken—and why aloud?—they stay in his mind as a key that does not work weighs heavily in a hand. And the figure of the tree splits, breaks apart, and comes together again higher up, in the absolute, as when one examines the warped glass in old windowpanes.

Color, pushed to the margins of the image by the swelling in the glass. What one ordinarily calls "form," now broken—denied—by a bulge. As if the hand pressing colors and forms together had opened.

III

Perdu. Et les choses accourent de toutes parts, se pressent autour de lui. Il n'y a plus d'ailleurs dans cet instant où il veut l'ailleurs, si intensément.

Mais le veut-il?

Et quelque chose accourt du centre même des choses. Il n'y a plus d'espace entre lui et la moindre chose.

Seule la montagne là-bas, très bleue, l'aide ici à respirer dans cette eau de ce qui est, qui remonte.

Familière pourtant cette impression d'une poussée qui s'exerce sur lui de par le dedans de tout. Hier, déjà, que de chemins trop abrupts vers le point de fuite, dans l'encre répandue des nuages! Que de mots qui venaient d'il ne savait où, parmi les mots! Que de ses jouets qui d'un seul coup n'étaient plus le petit damier ou les cubes couverts d'images mais le bois usé par le bord, la fibre qui perce la couleur!

On lui disait, de loin: Viens, et il n'entendait que cet éclaboussement du son qui se répand sur les dalles.

IV

Il se souvient qu'un oiseau avait marché devant lui tout un moment quand c'était le chemin encore.

Il va droit, depuis deux minutes. Mais le voici arrêté par de l'eau qui bouge parmi des souches. Il y a de la boue dans cette eau claire, une sorte de poudre bleue qui tourne sur soi là où le courant presque imperceptible frappe l'arête brillante d'une roche.

Lost. And things rush from everywhere, crowd around him. No longer is there an elsewhere in this instant when, so intensely, he desires the elsewhere.

But does he really desire it?

And something rushes out from the very center of things. No longer is there any space between him and the slightest thing.

Only the deeply blue mountain in the distance helps him breathe, here, in the rising water of what exists.

Familiar, however, is this impression of a force acting on him from within everything. Already yesterday, how many steep paths moving towards the vanishing point, in the spilled ink of clouds! How many words, appearing from he knew not where, among the words! How many of his playthings—the small checkerboard or the blocks covered with images—which, in an instant, were no longer toys but wood worn down along the edges, the grain showing through the paint!

From far away, they said to him, "Come," and he heard only a splatter of sound spreading over the flagstones.

IV

He remembers a bird walking in front of him for a while when he was still on the path.

Moving straight ahead for two minutes, he is now stopped by water rippling among the tree stumps. There is mud in this limpid water, a kind of blue powder turning on itself where the faint current strikes the shining edge of a rock.

S'il avait plu il retrouverait la trace de ses pas, mais la terre est sèche.

Le sentier qu'il avait suivi laissait le soleil à sa gauche. C'est là où il tournait qu'il y avait eu près du bord ces trois pierres tachées de blanc, comme peintes.

V

Mais pourquoi gravit-il maintenant cette butte presque escarpée, encore que les arbres y soient aussi serrés qu'en dessous, le long d'étroites ravines? Ce n'est sûrement pas par ici que le chemin passe.

Et ce n'est pas de là-haut qu'il aura vue.

Ni pourra crier son appel.

Je le vois qui monte pourtant parmi les fûts, dans les pierres.

S'aidant d'une branche basse quand il sent le sol trop glissant à cause des feuilles sèches parmi lesquelles il y a toujours ces cailloux roulant sur d'autres cailloux: losanges de bord acéré et de couleur grise, tachée de rouge.

Je le vois,—et j'imagine la cime. Quelques mètres d'à-plat, mais si indistincts du fait de ces ronces qui atteignent parfois aux branches. La même confusion, le même hasard que partout ailleurs dans le bois, mais ainsi en est-il pour tout ce qui vit. Un oiseau s'envole, qu'il ne voit pas. Un pin tombé une nuit de vent barre la pente qui recommence.

Et j'entends en moi cette voix, qui sourd du fond de l'enfance: Je suis venu ici, déjà—disait-elle alors—je connais ce lieu, j'y ai vécu, c'était avant le temps, c'était avant moi sur la terre.

Je suis le ciel, la terre.

Je suis le roi. Je suis ce tas de glands que le vent a poussés dans le creux qui est entre ces racines.

If it had rained, he would find the trace of his steps, but the earth is dry.

The sun had been on his left, as he followed the path. There, at a turning point of the path, three stones, spotted white as if painted, had rested near the edge.

V

But why does he now climb this steep slope, even though the trees are as dense as down below along the narrow ravines? The road surely does not pass this way.

And from up there he will not be able to see.

Or to call for help.

I see him climbing anyhow among the tree trunks, in the rocks.

He grabs hold of a low branch where the ground, covered by dry leaves and by loosened pebbles rolling over each other, becomes too slippery; the pebbles are diamond-shaped, their edges sharp, their color a gray, speckled with red.

I see him—and I imagine the hilltop. A few meters wide, but obscured by brambles, sometimes reaching the lower limbs of the trees. The same disorder and randomness as elsewhere in the woods, and as found in everything that lives. A bird flies off; he does not see it. A pine knocked down during a wind-tossed night blocks the slope, here rising again.

And I hear within me a voice welling up from the depths of childhood: "I've been here already," it said; "I know this place, I've lived here; it was before time, before my presence on earth.

"I am the sky, the earth.

"I am the king. I am this pile of acorns the wind has blown into the hollow between the roots."

Il a dix ans. L'âge où l'on regarde les ombres se déplacer, est-ce par saccades? et la déchirure dans le papier des murs, et le plâtre, et le clou planté dans le plâtre avec autour du métal rouillé les infimes écaillements de l'incompréhensible matière. S'est-il perdu? En fait, il avance depuis longtemps parmi de grandes énigmes. Il a toujours été seul. Il s'est assis sur l'arbre tombé, il pleure.

Perdu! C'est comme si l'au-delà que scelle le point de fuite venait se pencher sur lui, et le touchait à l'épaule.

Lever les yeux, alors. Quand deux directions sollicitent également, à un carrefour, le cœur bat plus fort et plus sourd, mais les yeux sont libres. Ce soir, à la maison, qu'il place des bûches sur le feu, comme on lui permet de le faire: il les verra brûler dans un autre monde.

Qu'il parle, pour lui seul: les mots retentiront dans un autre monde.

Et plus tard, bien plus tard, de longues années plus tard, seul, seul toujours dans sa chambre avec ce livre qu'il a écrit: il le prendra dans ses mains, regardera les lettres noires du titre sur le carton léger, teint de bleu. Il en séparera quelques pages, pour qu'il soit debout sur la table.

Puis il en approchera une allumette enflammée, une tache brune puis noire va naître dans la couleur, s'y élargira, se trouera, un liseré de feu clair en mordra les bords, qu'il écrasera du doigt avant de redresser la brochure pour réinscrire le signe à un autre endroit de la couverture. Voici maintenant que tout un coin de celle-ci est tombé. Le papier glacé, très blanc, de la première page, est apparu au dessous, atteint lui-même, jauni, par la chaleur.

Il pose le livre, il va garder en esprit, il ne sait encore pourquoi, le mariage des phrases et de la cendre.

He is ten. The age when one watches shadows as they move about by fits and starts, perhaps; when one watches the tear in the wallpaper and the plaster where the nail is embedded, its rusted metal surrounded by tiny flakes of an inscrutable substance. Was he lost? For a long time, indeed, he has been moving among great enigmas. He has always been alone. Seated on the fallen tree, he weeps.

Lost! It is as if the beyond to which the vanishing point attests came and leaned over him, touching him on the shoulder.

But he must look upward, now. When two routes beckon equally at a crossroads, the heart beats more strongly and more mutely, but the eyes are free. This evening, at home, let him put logs on the fire, as he has been permitted to do: he will see them burn in another world.

Let him speak, for himself alone: his words will echo in another world.

And later, much later, several long years later, alone, always alone in his room with the book he has written, he will take it in his hands and look at the black letters of the title on the thin, blue cover. He will remove some pages to make it stand on the table.

Then he will bring a lighted match close to it. A brown spot will appear in the color, turn black, widen, and become a hole. A border of bright fire will eat into the edges. He will rub it out with a finger, and then, having placed the book upright again, he will reinscribe the sign on another part of the cover. An entire corner falls off. The glossy white paper of the first page appears underneath, attacked and yellowed by the heat.

He puts the book down; although he does not yet know why, he will forever remember this marriage of words and ash.

L'aboi d'un chien, qui a mis fin à sa peur. Le pilier du soleil parmi les nuages, le soir. Les flaques que l'écolier voit étinceler dans les mots, dans l'à venir de sa vie, quand il pousse sa plume rêche dans l'enchevêtrement de la dictée trop rapide.

Et toute branche devant le ciel, à cause des évasements, des resserrements de sa masse. L'invisible qui là bouillonne, comme la source au dégel, violente. Et les baies rouges, parmi les feuilles.

Et la lumière, au retour; la flamme en quoi tout commence et tout prend fin.

The barking of a dog, which has ended his fear. Evening, a pillar of light among the clouds. Puddles, which the school-boy sees shimmering in the words, in the summons of his life, when he pushes his scratchy pen through the muddle of a too rapid dictation.

And every branch against the sky, its knotted surface widening or narrowing. The invisible that bubbles there furiously, like a melting spring at winter's end. And among the leaves, red berries.

And the light, upon his return; the flame wherein everything begins and comes to an end.

VII

Début et fin de la neige

■ ■ ■

The Beginning and the End of the Snow

1991
TRANSLATED BY RICHARD STAMELMAN
AND JOHN NAUGHTON

Qual si posava in terra, e qual su l'onde;
Qual con un vago errore
Girando parea dir: qui regna amore.

—Petrarch, *Il Canzioniere,* CXXVI

LA GRANDE NEIGE

Première neige tôt ce matin. L'ocre, le vert
Se réfugient sous les arbres.

Seconde, vers midi. Ne demeure
De la couleur
Que les aiguilles de pins
Qui tombent elles aussi plus dru parfois que la neige.

Puis, vers le soir,
Le fléau de la lumière s'immobilise.
Les ombres et les rêves ont même poids.

Un peu de vent
Écrit du bout du pied un mot hors du monde.

LE MIROIR

Hier encore
Les nuages passaient
Au fond noir de la chambre.
Mais à présent le miroir est vide.

Neiger
Se désenchevêtre du ciel.

THE HEAVY SNOW

First snow, early this morning. Green and ochre
Take refuge beneath the trees.

The second, around noon. Of color
There remain only
The pine needles
Falling more thickly at times than the snow.

Then, towards evening,
The scales of light tip no more.
Shadows and dreams have equal weight.

A light wind
Writes with the end of its foot a word beyond the world.

THE MIRROR

Yesterday, still,
Clouds passed
At the dark end of the room.
But now the mirror is empty.

Falling snow,
Disentangling from the sky.

LA CHARRUE

Cinq heures. La neige encore. J'entends des voix
À l'avant du monde.

Une charrue
Comme une lune au troisième quartier
Brille, mais la recouvre
La nuit d'un pli de la neige.

Et cet enfant
A toute la maison pour lui, désormais. Il va
D'une fenêtre à l'autre. Il presse
Ses doigts contre la vitre. Il voit
Des gouttes se former là où il cesse
D'en pousser la buée vers le ciel qui tombe.

LE PEU D'EAU

À ce flocon
Qui sur ma main se pose, j'ai désir
D'assurer l'éternel
En faisant de ma vie, de ma chaleur,
De mon passé, de ces jours d'à présent,
Un instant simplement: cet instant-ci, sans bornes.

Mais déjà il n'est plus
Qu'un peu d'eau, qui se perd
Dans la brume des corps qui vont dans la neige.

THE PLOW

Five o'clock. Snow again. I hear voices
At the bow of the world.

A field plow
Like a three-quarter moon
Shines, but night
Covers it in a fold of snow.

And the child,
The whole house to himself now,
Goes from window to window. He presses
His fingers against the glass, watching
Drops form where his hand no longer
Pushes the window's mist toward the falling sky.

THE DROP OF WATER

To this flake
Dropping on my finger, I wish
To grant eternity
By making of my life, my warmth,
My past, of all these present days,
Simply an instant: this one now, boundless.

But already it is no more
Than a drop of water, lost
In the mist of bodies moving through the snow.

sans titre

Neige
Fugace sur l'écharpe, sur le gant
Comme cette illusion, le coquelicot,
Dans la main qui rêva, l'été passé
Sur le chemin parmi les pierres sèches,
Que l'absolu est à portée du monde.

Pourtant, quelle promesse
Dans cette eau, de contact léger, puisqu'elle fut,
Un instant, la lumière! Le ciel d'été
N'a guère de nuées pour entrouvrir
Plus clair chemin sous des voûtes plus sombres.

Circé
Sous sa pergola d'ombres, l'illuminée,
N'eut pas de fruits plus rouges.

untitled

Snow,
Fleeting, on the scarf, the glove,
Like this illusion, a poppy
In the hand that last summer,
On a path among dry stones,
Dreamed the absolute was within the world's reach.

Yet, what promise
In the so gentle touch of this water, which
For an instant was light! The summer sky
Seldom has such clouds as shall open
A lighter path beneath darker vaults.

Circe, bathed in light,
Beneath her pergola of shadows,
Had no redder fruits than these.

LA VIERGE DE MISÉRICORDE

Tout, maintenant,
Bien au chaud
Sous ton manteau léger,
Presque rien que de brume et de broderie,
Madone de miséricorde de la neige.

Contre ton corps
Dorment, nus,
Les êtres et les choses, et tes doigts
Voilent de leur clarté ces paupières closes.

LE JARDIN

Il neige.
Sous les flocons la porte
Ouvre enfin au jardin
De plus que le monde.

J'avance. Mais se prend
Mon écharpe à du fer
Rouillé, et se déchire
En moi l'étoffe du songe.

LES POMMES

Et que faut-il penser
De ces pommes jaunes?
Hier, elles étonnaient, d'attendre ainsi, nues
Après la chute des feuilles,

Aujourd'hui elles charment
Tant leurs épaules
Sont, modestement, soulignées
D'un ourlet de neige.

THE VIRGIN OF MERCY

Everything, now,
So warm
Beneath your light coat,
Almost nothing but mist and embroidery,
Virgin of mercy of the snow.

Against your body,
Beings and things sleep
In nakedness, and the light
Of your fingers has veiled their closed eyelids.

THE GARDEN

It is snowing.
Beneath the flakes the door
Opens finally onto the garden
That is more than the world.

I walk on. But my scarf
Catches on a rusted
Fence, and the fabric
Of dreams tears within me.

APPLES

And what should we think
Of these yellow apples?
Yesterday, they surprised us,
Waiting like that, bare
After the leaves had fallen,

Today, they charm us,
Their shoulders so modestly
Enhanced by a fringe of snow.

J'avance dans la neige, j'ai fermé
Les yeux, mais la lumière sait franchir
Les paupières poreuses, et je perçois
Que dans mes mots c'est encore la neige
Qui tourbillonne, se resserre, se déchire.

Neige,
Lettre que l'on retrouve et que l'on déplie,
Et l'encre en a blanchi et dans les signes
La gaucherie de l'esprit est visible
Qui ne sait qu'en enchevêtrer les ombres claires.

Et on essaye de lire, on ne comprend pas
Qui s'intéresse à nous dans la mémoire,
Sinon que c'est l'été encore; et que l'on voit
Sous les flocons les feuilles, et la chaleur
Monter du sol absent comme une brume.

■ ■ ■

sans titre

On dirait beaucoup d'e muets dans une phrase.
On sent qu'on ne leur doit
Que des ombres de métaphores.

On dirait,
Dès qu'il neige plus dru,
De ces mains qui repoussent d'autres mains

Mais jouent avec les doigts qu'elles refusent.

SUMMER AGAIN

Walking through the snow, I close
My eyes, but light knows how to seep
Through porous eyelids, and in my words
I also see the snow
Whirling, thickening, scattering.

Snow.
A letter one finds again and unfolds,
Its ink has whitened, and in its signs
Is visible the awkwardness of the mind
That can only entangle their clear shadows.

And we try to read, not understanding
Who among our memories is thinking of us,
Except that it is summer again, and we see
Leaves beneath the flakes, and heat
Rising like mist from the absent ground.

■　■　■

untitled

You might say, a lot of silent *e*'s in a phrase.
You feel you owe them
Only a hint of metaphor.

You might say,
When the snowfall thickens,
Those hands that push other hands away

But play with the fingers they refuse.

sans titre

Flocons,
Bévues sans conséquences de la lumière.
L'une suit l'autre et d'autres encore, comme si
Comprendre ne comptait plus, rire davantage.

Et Aristote le disait bien,
Quelque part dans sa Poétique *qu'on lit si mal,*
C'est la transparence qui vaut,
Dans des phrases qui soient comme une rumeur d'abeilles, comme
    une eau claire.

DE NATURA RERUM

Lucrèce le savait:
Ouvre le coffre,
Tu verras, il est plein de neige
Qui tourbillonne.

Et parfois deux flocons
Se rencontrent, s'unissent,
Ou bien l'un se détourne, gracieusement
Dans son peu de mort.

D'où vient qu'il fasse clair
Dans quelques mots
Quand l'un n'est que la nuit,
L'autre, qu'un rêve?

D'où viennent ces deux ombres
Qui vont, riant,
Et l'une emmitouflée
D'une laine rouge?

untitled

Snowflakes,
Harmless blunders of light.
One follows another, and still others,
As though understanding no longer mattered,
Only laughter.

Aristotle put it well
Somewhere in his *Poetics* which we read so poorly,
It is the transparency that counts
In phrases that are like the buzzing of bees, like clear water.

DE NATURA RERUM

Lucretius knew this:
Open the chest,
You shall see, it is full of
Whirling snow.

And, sometimes two flakes
Meet, unite,
Or else one turns away, gracefully,
Into its humble death.

How is it that daylight shines
In some words
When one is only night,
The other, dream?

From where do these two shadows come
That advance, laughing,
One muffled in
A scarf of red wool?

LA PARURE

Il neige. Âme, que voulais-tu
Que tu n'aies eu de naissance éternelle?
Vois, tu as là
Pour la mort même une robe de fête.

Une parure comme à l'adolescence,
De celles que l'on prend à mains soucieuses
Car l'étoffe en est transparente et reste près
Des doigts qui la déploient dans la lumière,
On sait qu'elle est fragile comme l'amour.

Mais des corolles, des feuilles y sont brodées,
Et déjà la musique se fait entendre
Dans la salle voisine, illuminée.
Une ardeur mystérieuse te prend la main.

Tu vas, le cœur battant, dans la grande neige.

NOLI ME TANGERE

Hésite le flocon dans le ciel bleu
À nouveau, le dernier flocon de la grande neige.

Et c'est comme entrerait au jardin celle qui
Avait bien dû rêver ce qui pourrait être,
Ce regard, ce dieu simple, sans souvenir
Du tombeau, sans pensée que le bonheur,
Sans avenir
Que sa dissipation dans le bleu du monde.

«Non, ne me touche pas», lui dirait-il,
Mais même dire non serait de lumière.

ELEGANCE

It is snowing. Soul, what have you wanted
That you did not have from eternal birth?
Look, even for death
You have this festive gown.

A dress like those of adolescence,
Which you took in careful hands,
For the material is transparent and clings to
The fingers unfurling it in the light,
One knows that it is delicate like love.

But petals and leaves are embroidered in it,
And already a music can be heard
In the next room, brightly lit.
A mysterious fervor takes you by the hand.

You go out, with beating heart, into the heavy snow.

NOLI ME TANGERE

Hesitant the snowflake across the sky
Turned blue, the last flake of the heavy snow.

And it is as though she had come into the garden,
The one who had surely dreamed of what could be,
This look, this simple god, with no memory
Of the grave, with no thought but happiness,
With no future
But his dissipation in the blue of the world.

"No, do not touch me," he would say to her,
But even such refusal would have a light all its own.

sans titre

Juste avant l'aube
Je regarde à travers les vitres, et je crois comprendre
Qu'il a cessé de neiger. Une flaque bleue
S'étend, brillante un peu, devant les arbres,
D'une paroi à l'autre de la nuit.

Je sors.
Je descends précautionneusement l'escalier de bois
Dont les marches sont nivelées par la neige fraîche.
Le froid cerne et pénètre mes chevilles,
Il semble que l'esprit en soit plus clair,
Qui perçoit mieux le silence des choses.

Dort-il encore
Dans l'enchevêtrement du tas de bois
Serré sous la fenêtre,
Le chipmunk, notre voisin simple,
Ou est-il déjà à errer dans les crissements et le froid?
Je vois d'infimes marques devant la porte.

untitled

Just before dawn
I look out the windows and think
It has stopped snowing. A blue puddle,
Gleaming faintly in front of the trees, stretches
From one wall of the night to the other.

I go out.
Cautiously, I descend the wooden staircase,
Its steps made level by the fresh snow.
The cold surrounds and penetrates my ankles,
And thus, the mind, it seems, becomes clearer,
Sensing more deeply the silence of things.

Is the chipmunk,
Our simple neighbor, still asleep
In the jumbled heap of logs
Packed beneath the window,
Or is he already out wandering in the crunching snow and the
    cold?
I see tiny marks before the door.

[R.S.]

LES FLAMBEAUX

Neige
Qui as cessé de donner, qui n'es plus
Celle qui vient mais celle qui attend
En silence, ayant apporté mais sans qu'encore
On ait pris, et pourtant, tout la nuit,
Nous avons aperçu, dans l'embuement
Des vitres parfois même ruisselantes,
Ton étincellement sur la grande table.

Neige, notre chemin,
Immaculé encore, pour aller prendre
Sous les branches courbées et comme attentives
Ces flambeaux, ce qui est, qui ont paru
Un à un, et brûlé, mais semblent s'éteindre
Comme aux yeux du désir quand il accède
Aux biens dont il rêvait (car c'est souvent
Quand tout se dénouerait peut-être, que s'efface
En nous de salle en salle le reflet
Du ciel, dans les miroirs), ô neige, touche

Encore ces flambeaux, renflamme-les
Dans le froid de cette aube; et qu'à l'exemple
De tes flocons qui déjà les assaillent
De leur insouciance, feu plus clair,
Et malgré tant de fièvre dans la parole
Et tant de nostalgie dans le souvenir,
Nos mots ne cherchent plus les autres mots mais les avoisinent,
Passent auprès d'eux, simplement,
Et si l'un en a frôlé un, et s'ils s'unissent,
Ce ne sera qu'encore ta lumière,
Notre brièveté qui se dissémine,
L'écriture qui se dissipe, sa tâche faite.

THE TORCHES

Snow
That has stopped giving, that is no longer
The one who comes but the one who waits
In silence, having brought what has not yet
Been taken, even though, all through the night
We noticed, in the mist of the windowpanes
That sometimes were streaming with water,
Your glimmering on the wide table.

Snow, our path,
Still immaculate, for going to take
Beneath branches that were bowed down, attentive,
These torches, what is, that appeared
One by one, and burned, but seem to go out
As in the eyes of desire when it reaches
The gifts it had dreamed of (for it is often
When everything might perhaps be resolved
That from room to room in us the reflection
Of the sky dies out in the mirrors), oh snow, touch

Once more these torches, rekindle them
In the cold of this dawn; and following the example
Of your flakes that already assail them
With their carefreeness, brighter fire,
And in spite of so much fever in speech,
And so much nostalgia in memory,
May our words no longer seek other words, but neighbor them,
Draw beside them, simply,
And if one has brushed another, if they unite,
This will still be only your light,
Our brevity scattering,
Our writing dissipating, its task finished.

(Et tel flocon s'attarde, on le suit des yeux,
On aimerait le regarder toujours,
Tel autre s'est posé sur la main offerte.

Et tel plus lent et comme égaré s'éloigne
Et tournoie, puis revient. Et n'est-ce dire
Qu'un mot, un autre mot encore, à inventer,
Rédimerait le monde? Mais on ne sait
Si on entend ce mot ou si on le rêve.)

(And here a snowflake lingers, our eyes follow it,
We would love to look at it forever,
Here another falls upon the open hand.

And here another, slower and as though lost, goes off,
Turns about, then comes back. And isn't this to say
That a word, yet another word, still to be invented,
Might redeem the world? But one never knows
If this word is heard or only dreamed of.)

[J.N.]

HOPKINS FOREST

J'étais sorti
Prendre de l'eau au puits, auprès des arbres,
Et je fus en présence d'un autre ciel.
Disparues les constellations d'il y a un instant encore,
Les trois quarts du firmament étaient vides,
Le noir le plus intense y régnait seul,
Mais à gauche, au-dessus de l'horizon,
Mêlé à la cime des chênes,
Il y avait un amas d'étoiles rougeoyantes
Comme un brasier, d'où montait même une fumée.

Je rentrai
Et je rouvris le livre sur la table.
Page après page,
Ce n'étaient que des signes indéchiffrables,
Des agrégats de formes d'aucun sens
Bien que vaguement récurrentes,
Et par-dessous une blancheur d'abîme
Comme si ce qu'on nomme l'esprit tombait là, sans bruit,
Comme une neige.
Je tournai cependant les pages.

Bien des années plus tôt,
Dans un train au moment où le jour se lève
Entre Princeton Junction et Newark,
C'est-à-dire deux lieux de hasard pour moi,
Deux retombées des flèches de nulle part,
Les voyageurs lisaient, silencieux
Dans la neige qui balayait les vitres grises,
Et soudain,
Dans un journal ouvert à deux pas de moi,
Une grande photographie de Baudelaire,
Toute une page
Comme le ciel se vide à la fin du monde
Pour consentir au désordre des mots.

HOPKINS FOREST

I had gone out
To take water from the well, near the trees,
And then, the fall presence of another sky.
Gone were the constellations from a moment before,
Three quarters of the firmament were empty,
Utter darkness reigned alone,
But on the left, above the horizon,
Blending with the tops of the oaks,
There was a pile of stars blazing
Like coals, and smoke was even rising from them.

I went back in
And reopened the book on the table,
Page after page,
Nothing but indecipherable signs,
Aggregates of meaningless forms
Though vaguely recurrent,
And beneath them the white of an abyss
As though what we call mind were falling there,
Soundlessly,
Like snow.
And yet, I turned the pages.

Many years earlier,
On a train as day was breaking
Between Princeton Junction and Newark,
That is, two random places for me,
The fall of two arrows from nowhere,
The passengers were reading in silence
As the snow swept the gray windows,
And all at once,
In a newspaper a few feet away,
A huge photograph of Baudelaire,
A whole page,
As the sky empties at the end of the world
To accept the disorder of words.

J'ai rapproché ce rêve et ce souvenir
Quand j'ai marché, d'abord tout un automne
Dans des bois où bientôt ce fut la neige
Qui triompha, dans beaucoup de ces signes
Que l'on reçoit, contradictoirement,
Du monde dévasté par le langage.
Prenait fin le conflit de deux principes,
Me semblait-il, se mêlaient deux lumières,
Se refermaient les lèvres de la plaie.
La masse blanche du froid tombait par rafales
Sur la couleur, mais un toit au loin, une planche
Peinte, restée debout contre une grille,
C'était encore la couleur, et mystérieuse
Comme un qui sortirait du sépulcre et, riant:
«Non, ne me touche pas», dirait-il au monde.

Je dois vraiment beaucoup à Hopkins Forest,
Je la garde à mon horizon, dans sa partie
Qui quitte le visible pour l'invisible
Par le tressaillement du bleu des lointains.
Je l'écoute, à travers les bruits, et parfois même,
L'été, poussant du pied les feuilles mortes
D'autres années, claires dans la pénombre
Des chênes trop serrés parmi les pierres,
Je m'arrête, je crois que ce sol s'ouvre
À l'infini, que ces feuilles y tombent
Sans hâte, ou bien remontent, le haut, le bas
N'étant plus, ni le bruit, sauf le léger
Chuchotement des flocons qui bientôt
Se multiplient, se rapprochent, se nouent
—Et je revois alors tout l'autre ciel,
J'entre pour un instant dans la grande neige.

I brought together this dream and this memory
When I walked, at first all through autumn
In woods where snow was soon
To triumph in many of those signs
One receives, so often in contradiction,
From the world devastated by language.
It seemed that the conflict between two principles
Was coming to an end, two lights were mingling,
The lips of the wound were closing.
The white mass of the cold fell in gusts
Upon the color, but a roof in the distance,
A painted board, resting against a gate,
This was still color, and mysterious,
Like someone who would rise up from a sepulchre
And, smiling, say to the world:
"No, do not touch me."

I really owe a lot to Hopkins Forest,
I keep it on my horizon, the part of it
That leaves the visible for the invisible
Through the quivering of the blue in the distant background.
I listen to it, through the sounds, and sometimes even,
In summer, my foot pushing the dead leaves
Of other years, bright in the half light
Of the oaks too tightly clustered among the stones,
I stop, I think that this ground is opening to
The infinite, that these leaves are falling there
Without haste, or else are rising upwards, down, up,
No longer existing, nor any sound, except the gentle
Whispering of the snowflakes that soon
Multiply, draw together, join to one another
—And then I see once more the whole other sky,
And enter for awhile the great heavy snow.

[J.N.]

LE TOUT, LE RIEN

I

C'est la dernière neige de la saison,
La neige de printemps, la plus habile
À recoudre les déchirures du bois mort
Avant qu'on ne l'emporte puis le brûle.

C'est la première neige de ta vie
Puisque, hier, ce n'étaient encore que des taches
De couleur, plaisirs brefs, craintes, chagrins
Inconsistants, faute de la parole.

Et je vois que la joie prend sur la peur
Dans tes yeux que dessille la surprise
Une avance, d'un grand bond clair: ce cri, ce rire
Que j'aime, et que je trouve méditable.

Car nous sommes bien proches, et l'enfant
Est le progéniteur de qui l'a pris
Un matin dans ses mains d'adulte et soulevé
Dans le consentement de la lumière.

II

Oui, à entendre, oui, à faire mienne
Cette source, le cri de joie, qui bouillonnante
Surgit d'entre les pierres de la vie
Tôt, et si fort, puis faiblit et s'aveugle.

Mais écrire n'est pas avoir, ce n'est pas être,
Car le tressaillement de la joie n'y est
Qu'une ombre, serait-elle la plus claire,
Dans des mots qui encore se souviennent

THE WHOLE, THE NOTHINGNESS

I

It's the last snow of the year,
Spring snow, the best able
To sew up the tears in the dead wood
Before it's taken off to be burned.

It's the first snow of your life
Since, yesterday, there were still only spots
Of color, brief pleasures, fears, sorrows,
Lacking in consistency, since lacking in speech.

And in your eyes that surprise has opened,
I can see joy leaving fear behind
In a bright bound: this cry, this laughter
That I love, and that I find ponderable.

For we are very close, and the child
Is the progenitor of the man who took him up
One morning in his grownup hands and lifted him
Into the light's consenting.

II

Yes, at understanding, yes, at making mine
This spring, the cry of joy, that surges up
Bubbling over among the stones of life
Early and strong, then weakens and goes blind.

But to write is not to have, is not to be,
For the quiver of any joy is only
A shadow there, though sometimes so bright
In words that still remember

De tant et tant de choses que le temps
A durement labourées de ses griffes,
—Et je ne puis donc faire que te dire
Ce que je ne suis pas, sauf en désir.

Une façon de prendre, qui serait
De cesser d'être soi dans l'acte de prendre,
Une façon de dire, qui ferait
Qu'on ne serait plus seul dans le langage.

III

Te soit la grande neige le tout, le rien,
Enfant des premiers pas titubants dans l'herbe,
Les yeux encore pleins de l'origine,
Les mains ne s'agrippant qu'à la lumière.

Te soient ces branches qui scintillent la parole
Que tu dois écouter mais sans comprendre
Le sens de leur découpe sur le ciel,
Sinon tu ne dénommerais qu'au prix de perdre.

Te suffisent les deux valeurs, l'une brillante,
De la colline dans l'échancrure des arbres,
Abeille de la vie, quand se tarira
Dans ton rêve du monde ce monde même.

Et que l'eau qui ruisselle dans le pré
Te montre que la joie peut survivre au rêve
Quand la brise d'on ne sait où venue déjà disperse
Les fleurs de l'amandier, pourtant l'autre neige.

So many, many things that time
Has roughly ploughed with its claws,
—And thus all I can do is tell you
What I'm not, except in desire.

A way of taking, that would be
To cease being a self in the act of taking,
A way among the words, that would be
The end of our solitude in language.

III

May the great snow be the whole, the nothingness,
Child, trying your first unsteady steps in the grass,
Your eyes still full of origin,
Your hands clinging to nothing but the light.

May these branches that sparkle be the words
You must listen to but without understanding
The meaning of their pattern on the sky,
Since anything you name you might destroy.

May the two lines (one bright) of the hill
In the opening between the trees be enough for you,
Bee of life, when in your dream of the world
This world itself ceases to be.

And may the water that runs in the meadow
Show you that joy can survive dream
When the breeze that comes from we know not where
Scatters the almond tree's flowers, this other snow.

[J.N.]

LA SEULE ROSE

Il neige, c'est revenir dans une ville
Où, et je le découvre en avançant
Au hasard dans des rues qui toutes sont vides,
J'aurais vécu heureux une autre enfance.
Sous les flocons j'aperçois des façades
Qui ont beauté plus que rien de ce monde.
Seuls parmi nous Alberti puis San Gallo
À San Biagio, dans la salle la plus intense
Qu'ait bâtie le désir, ont approché
De cette perfection, de cette absence.

Et je regarde donc, avidement,
Ces masses que la neige me dérobe.
Je recherche surtout, dans la blancheur
Errante, ces frontons que je vois qui montent
À un plus haut niveau de l'apparence.
Ils déchirent la brume, c'est comme si
D'une main délivrée de la pesanteur
L'architecte d'ici avait fait vivre
D'un seul grand trait floral
La forme que voulait de siècle en siècle
La douleur d'être né dans la matière.

THE ONLY ROSE

I

It's snowing, it's returning to a town
Where, as I discover as I go through
Empty streets I come upon by chance,
I might have happily lived some other childhood.
Beneath the snowflakes I notice façades
More beautiful than anything in this world.
Among us, only Alberti, then Sangallo,
At San Biagio, in the most intense room
That desire has ever built, have approached
This perfection, this absence.

And so I gaze avidly
At these masses the snow hides from me.
I seek, above all, in the wandering
Whiteness, those pediments that rise
To a higher level of appearance.
They tear apart the mist, it is as though,
With a hand freed from weight,
The mortal architect had brought to life,
In a single floral stroke,
The form sought for centuries by
The pain of being born into matter.

II

Et là-haut je ne sais si c'est la vie
Encore, ou la joie seule, qui se détache
Sur ce ciel qui n'est plus de notre monde.
O bâtisseurs
Non tant d'un lieu que d'un regain de l'espérance,
Qu'y a-t-il au secret de ces parois
Qui devant moi s'écartent? Ce que je vois
Le long des murs, ce sont des niches vides,
Des pleins et des déliés, d'où s'évapore
Par la grâce des nombres
Le poids de la naissance dans l'exil,
Mais de la neige s'y est mise et s'y entasse,
Je m'approche de l'une d'elles, la plus basse,
Je fais tomber un peu de sa lumière,
Et soudain c'est le pré de mes dix ans,
Les abeilles bourdonnent,
Ce que j'ai dans mes mains, ces fleurs, ces ombres,
Est-ce presque du miel, est-ce de la neige?

III

J'avance alors, jusque sous l'arche d'une porte.
Les flocons tourbillonnent, effaçant
La limite entre le dehors et cette salle
Où des lampes sont allumées: mais elles-mêmes
Une sorte de neige, qui hésite
Entre le haut, le bas, dans cette nuit.
C'est comme si j'étais sur un second seuil.

II

And up there I cannot tell if it is still
Life, or only joy, that stands out
Against this sky no longer of our world.
Oh you builders,
Not so much of place as of renewed hope,
What is there in the depths of these walls
That open before me? What I see
Along the walls are only empty niches,
Partly stone, partly the absence of stone,
From which, thanks to symmetry,
The weight of being born into exile is lifted.
But snow has gathered there, has piled up,
I draw near to one of them, the lowest,
I bring down a bit of its light
And all at once it is the meadow I walked in at ten,
The bees are buzzing,
What I have in my hands, these flowers, these shadows,
Is it almost honey, is it snow?

III

And then I go on until I am beneath an archway,
The snowflakes are swirling, blotting out
The line between the outside and this room
Where lamps are lit: these, too,
A kind of snow, which hesitates
Between the high and the low, in this night.
It is as though I were at a second threshold.

Et au-delà ce même bruit d'abeilles
Dans le bruit de la neige. Ce que disaient
Les abeilles sans nombre de l'été,
Semble le refléter l'infini des lampes.

Et je voudrais
Courir, comme du temps de l'abeille, cherchant
Du pied la balle souple, car peut-être
Je dors, et rêve, et vais par les chemins d'enfance.

IV

Mais ce que je regarde, c'est de la neige
Durcie, qui s'est glissée sur le dallage
Et s'accumule aux bases des colonnes
À gauche, à droite, et loin devant dans la pénombre.
Absurdement je n'ai d'yeux que pour l'arc
Que cette boue dessine sur la pierre.
J'attache ma pensée à ce qui n'a
Pas de nom, pas de sens. Ô mes amis,
Alberti, Brunelleschi, San Gallo,
Palladio qui fais signe de l'autre rive,
Je ne vous trahis pas, cependant, j'avance,
La forme la plus pure reste celle
Qu'a pénétrée la brume qui s'efface,
La neige piétinée est la seule rose.

And beyond, the same sound of bees
In the sound of the snow. What the countless
Summer bees were saying
Seems reflected in the infinite of the lamps.

And I would like
To run, as in the time of the bee, seeking
With my foot the supple ball, for perhaps
I am sleeping, and dreaming, and wandering along
The paths of childhood.

IV

But what I am looking at is hardened snow,
The flakes which have stolen onto the flagstones
And piled up at the base of the columns
Left and right, and far ahead in the dusk.
Absurdly, my eyes can only see the arc
That this mud draws on the stone.
My only thought is for what has
No name, no meaning. Oh my friends,
Alberti, Brunelleschi, Sangallo,
Palladio who beckons from the other shore,
I do not betray you, I still go forward,
The purest form is always the one
Pierced by the mist that fades away,
Trampled snow is the only rose.

[J.N.]

VIII

La Vie errante

. . .

The Wandering Life

1993
TRANSLATED BY JOHN NAUGHTON

DE VENT ET DE FUMÉE

I

L'Idée, a-t-on pensé, est la mesure de tout,
D'où suit que «la sua bella Elena rapita», dit Bellori
D'une célèbre peinture de Guido Reni,
Peut être comparée à l'autre Hélène,
Celle qu'imagina, aima peut-être, Zeuxis.
Mais que sont des images auprès de la jeune femme
Que Pâris a tant désirée? La seule vigne,
N'est-ce pas le frémissement des mains réelles
Sous la fièvre des lèvres? Et que l'enfant
Demande avidement à la grappe, et boive
À même la lumière, en hâte, avant
Que le temps ne déferle sur ce qui est?

Mais non,
A pensé un commentateur de l'Iliade, anxieux
D'expliquer, d'excuser dix ans de guerre,
Et le vrai, c'est qu'Hélène ne fut pas
Assaillie, ne fut pas transportée de barque en vaisseau,
Ne fut pas retenue, criante, enchaînée
Sur des lits en désordre. Le ravisseur
N'emportait qu'une image: une statue
Que l'art d'un magicien avait faite des brises
Des soirées de l'été quand tout est calme,
Pour qu'elle eût la tiédeur du corps en vie
Et même sa respiration, et le regard
Qui se prête au désir. La feinte Hélène
Erre rêveusement sous les voûtes basses
Du navire qui fuit, il semble qu'elle écoute
Le bruit de l'autre mer dans ses veines bleues
Et qu'elle soit heureuse. D'autres scoliastes
Ont même cru à une œuvre de pierre.
Dans la cabine
Jour après jour secouée par le gros temps
Hélène est figurée, à demi levée

WIND AND SMOKE

I

The idea, it was thought, is the measure of everything,
From which it follows that "la sua bella Elena rapita,"
As Bellori said of a famous painting by Guido Reni,
Might be compared to that other Helen,
The one imagined, loved perhaps, by Zeuxis.
But what are images next to the young woman
Who filled Paris with such desire? The only vine,
Is it not the trembling of real hands
Beneath the fever of ardent lips? Is it not the child
Who asks avidly of the grape and who drinks,
In haste, straight from the light
Before time surges back over what is?

That's not it,
A commentator on the Illiad maintained,
Anxious to explain, to justify, ten years of war,
The truth is that Helen was never sprung upon,
Was never transported from boat to ship,
Was never held captive, screaming, chained
On crumpled beds. Her abductor
Carried off only an image: a statue
That a magician's art had made of the breezes
Of summer evenings when all is calm,
So she would have the warmth of a living body
And even its breathing, and the look
That lends itself to desire. The pretend Helen
Wanders dreamily beneath the low arches
Of the fleeing ship, she seems to listen to
The sounds of the other sea in her blue veins
And to be happy. Other Scholiasts
Have even believed in a work in stone.
In her cabin
Shaken day after day by rough weather
Helen is represented half risen

De ses draps, de ses rêves,
Elle sourit, ou presque. Son bras est reployé
Avec beaucoup de grâce sur son sein,
Les rayons du soleil, levant, couchant,
S'attardent puis s'effacent sur son flanc nu.
Et plus tard, sur la terrasse de Troie,
Elle a toujours ce sourire.
Qui pourtant, sauf Pâris peut-être, l'a jamais vue?
Les porteurs n'auront su que la grande pierre rougeâtre,
Rugueuse, fissurée
Qu'il leur fallut monter, suant, jurant,
Jusque sur les remparts, devant la nuit.

Cette roche,
Ce sable de l'origine, qui se délite,
Est-ce Hélène? Ces nuages, ces lueurs rouges
On ne sait si dans l'âme ou dans le ciel?

La vérité peut-être, mais gardée tue,
Même Stésichorus ne l'avoue pas,
Voici: la semblance d'Hélène ne fut qu'un feu
Bâti contre le vent sur une plage.
C'est une masse de branches grises, de fumées
(Car le feu prenait mal) que Pâris a chargée
Au petit jour humide sur la barque.
C'est ce brasier, ravagé par les vagues,
Cerné par le clameur des oiseaux de mer,
Qu'il restitua au monde, sur les brisants
Du rivage natal, que ravagent et trouent
D'autres vagues encore. Le lit de pierre
Avait été dressé là-haut, de par le ciel,
Et quand Troie tomberait resterait le feu
Pour crier la beauté, la protestation de l'esprit
Contre la mort.

Nuées,
L'une qui prend à l'autre, qui défend
Mal, qui répand
Entre ces corps épris
La coupe étincelante de la foudre.

From her sheets, from her dreams,
Smiling, or almost. Her arm is bent
With charming grace over her breast,
The rays of the sun, rising, setting,
Linger upon, then withdraw from her naked flank.
And later, on the terrace of Troy,
She always has this smile.
Who, though, aside from Paris perhaps, has ever seen her?
The slaves will only have known the reddish stone,
Rough, cracked,
That they had to carry up, sweating, cursing,
To the top of the ramparts, facing the night.

This rock,
This sand from the origin of Time, crumbling,
Is it Helen? These clouds, these gleams of red,
We don't know whether in the soul or in the sky?

The truth perhaps, though never spoken,
Not even Stesichorus admits it,
Is this: the semblance of Helen was only a fire
Built against the wind on a beach.
It is simply a mass of gray branches, of smoke
(For the fire was hard to start) that Paris loaded
Onto a boat at daybreak, when it was damp.
It is this brazier, ravaged by the waves,
Surrounded by the clamor of the sea birds,
That he restored to the world, on the shoals
Of the native shore, torn and pierced
By yet other waves. The bed of stone
Had been erected up there, near the sky,
And should Troy fall this fire would remain
To cry out beauty and the spirit's protest
Against death.

Clouds,
And one that takes from the other, that tries
To hold on, spilling
Between these bodies in love
The dazzling cup of the lightning.

Et le ciel
S'est attardé, un peu,
Sur la couche terrestre. On dirait, apaisés,
L'homme, la femme: une montagne, une eau.
Entre eux
La coupe déjà vide, encore pleine.

II

Mais qui a dit
Que celle que Pâris a étreint, le feu,
Les branches rouges dans le feu, l'âcre fumée
Dans les orbites vides, ne fut pas même
Ce rêve, qui se fait œuvre pour calmer
Le désir de l'artiste, mais simplement
Un rêve de ce rêve? Le sourire d'Hélène:
Rien que ce glissement du drap de la nuit, qui montre,
Mais pour rien qu'un éclair,
La lumière endormie en bas du ciel.

Chaque fois qu'un poème,
Une statue, même une image peinte,
Se préfèrent figure, se dégagent
Des à-coups d'étincellement de la nuée,
Hélène se dissipe, qui ne fut
Que l'intuition qui fit se pencher Homère
Sur des sons de plus bas que ses cordes dans
La maladroite lyre des mots terrestres.

Mais à l'aube du sens
Quand la pierre est encore obscure, la couleur
Boue, dans l'impatience du pinceau,
Pâris emporte Hélène,
Elle se débat, elle crie,
Elle accepte; et les vagues sont calmes, contre l'étrave,
Et l'aube est rayonnante sur la mer.

Afterwards, the sky
Lingered for a moment
Over the earthly bed. You might say
A man and a woman, at peace: a mountain, water.
Between them
The cup already empty, still full.

II

But who has said
That the one embraced by Paris, the fire,
The red branches in the fire, the acrid smoke
In the empty sockets, was not even
That dream that wants to be a work of art to calm
The artist's longing, but rather, simply,
A dream of this dream? Helen's smile:
Nothing but that slipping of night's sheet, that reveals,
But only for a lightning flash,
The light sleeping at the base of the sky.

Every time that a poem,
A statue, even a painted image,
Prefers itself as form, breaks away
From the cloud's sudden jolts of sparkling light,
Helen vanishes, who was only
That intuition which led Homer to bend
Over sounds that come from lower than his strings
In the clumsy lyre of earthly words.

But at the dawn of meaning
When the stone is still in darkness, color
Only mud, in the brush's impatience,
Paris carries off Helen,
She struggles, she cries out,
She surrenders; and the waves are calm, against the bow,
And dawn is radiant on the sea.

Bois, dit Pâris
Qui s'éveille, et étend le bras dans l'ombre étroite
De la chambre remuée par le peu de houle,
Bois,
Puis approche la coupe de mes lèvres
Pour que je puisse boire.

Je me penche, répond
Celle qui est, peut-être, ou dont il rêve.
Je me penche, je bois,
Je n'ai pas plus de nom que la nuée,
Je me déchire comme elle, lumière pure.

Et t'ayant donné joie je n'ai plus de soif,
Lumière bue.

C'est un enfant
Nu sur la grande plage quand Troie brûlait
Que le dernier vit Hélène
Dans les buissons de flammes du haut des murs.
Il errait, il chantait,
Il avait pris dans ses mains un peu d'eau,
Le feu venait y boire, mais l'eau s'échappe
De la coupe imparfaite, ainsi le temps
Ruine le rêve et pourtant le rédime.

III

Ces pages sont traduites. D'une langue
Qui hante la mémoire que je suis.
Les phrases de cette langue sont incertaines
Comme les tout premiers de nos souvenirs.
J'ai restitué le texte mot après mot,
Mais le mien n'en sera qu'une ombre, c'est à croire
Que l'origine est une Troie qui brûle,
La beauté un regret, l'œuvre ne prendre
À pleines mains qu'une eau qui se refuse.

Drink, says Paris,
Who awakens, and stretches out his arm into the narrow
Shadow of the room rocked by the water's gentle swell,
Drink,
Then bring the cup to my lips
So that I can drink.

I bend down, answers
She who is perhaps, or of whom he dreams.
I bend down, I drink,
I have no more name than the cloud does,
I tear apart as it does, pure light.

And having given you joy, I have no more thirst,
Light drunk.

It is a naked
Child on the great beach when Troy was burning
Who was the last to see Helen
In the thickets of flame at the height of the walls.
He was roaming, singing,
He had taken in his hands a little water,
The fire came to drink there, but the water
Leaked out from the imperfect cup, just as time
Ruins dreams and yet redeems them.

III

These pages are translated. From a language
That haunts the memory that I am.
The phrases of this language are uncertain
Like the very first of our recollections.
I have reconstructed the text one word after another,
But mine can only be a shadow of the first one.
Must we feel: origin is a burning Troy,
Beauty is regretting, art is gathering up
By the handful nothing but absent water?

SELECTED BIBLIOGRAPHY

PRINCIPAL WORKS OF YVES BONNEFOY:

Poems:

Du mouvement et de l'immobilité de Douve, Mercure de France, 1953.

Hier régnant désert, Mercure de France, 1958.

Pierre écrite, Mercure de France, 1965.

Dans le leurre du seuil, Mercure de France, 1975.

Poèmes (1947–1975), Mercure de France, 1978 (Collection Poésie, Gallimard, 1982).

Ce qui fut sans lumière, Mercure de France, 1987.

Début et fin de la neige, followed by *Là où retombe la flèche,* Mercure de France, 1991.

Prose:

L'Arrière-pays, Skira, 1972 (Flammarion, 1982).

L'Ordalie, Galerie Maeght, 1974.

Rue Traversière, Mercure de France, 1977.

Récits en rêve, Mercure de France, 1987.

Rue Traversière et autres récits en rêve, Collection Poésie, Gallimard, 1992.

Remarques sur le dessin, Mercure de France, 1993.

La Vie errante, Mercure de France, 1993.

Criticism and Art History:

Peintures murales de la France gothique, Paul Hartmann, 1954.

L'Improbable, Mercure de France, 1959.

Arthur Rimbaud, Le Seuil, 1961.

Un Rêve fait à Mantoue, Mercure de France, 1967.

Rome 1630: l'horizon du premier baroque, Flammarion, 1970.

Le Nuage rouge, Mercure de France, 1977.

L'Improbable, followed by *Un Rêve fait à Mantoue,* revised and expanded edition, Mercure de France, 1980 (Collection Folio, Essais Gallimard, 1992).

Leçon inaugurale de la chaire d'Etudes comparées de la fonction poétique, Collège de France, 1982 (*La Présence et l'image,* Mercure de France, 1983).

La Vérité de parole, Mercure de France, 1988.

Sur un sculpteur et des peintres, Plon, 1989.

Entretiens sur la poésie, Mercure de France, 1990.

Alberto Giacometti, Flammarion, 1991.

Translations:

Henry IV (I); Jules César; Hamlet; Le Conte d'hiver; Vénus et Adonis; Le Viol de Lucrèce, Club Français du Livre, 1957–1960.

Jules César, Mercure de France, 1960.

Hamlet, followed by "Une Idée de la traduction," Mercure de France, 1962 (new edition, 1988).

Le Roi Lear, Mercure de France, 1965 (new edition, 1991, preceded by "Comment traduire Shakespeare?").

Roméo et Juliette, Mercure de France, 1968.

Hamlet/Le Roi Lear, preceded by "Readiness, Ripeness: Hamlet, Lear," Gallimard, Collection Folio, 1978 (new edition, Mercure de France, 1988).

Macbeth, Mercure de France, 1983.

Roméo et Juliette/MacBeth, preceded by "L'Inquiétude de Shakespeare," Gallimard, Collection Folio, 1985.

Quarante-cinq poèmes de Yeats, followed by *Résurrection,* Hermann, 1989.

Les Poèmes de Shakespeare, preceded by "Traduire en vers ou en prose," Mercure de France, 1993.

Le Conte d'hiver, preceded by "'Art et Nature': l'arrière-plan du *Conte d'hiver,*" Mercure de France, 1994.

Jules César, preceded by "Brutus, ou le rendez-vous à Philippes," Mercure de France, 1995.

Edited Work:

Dictionnaire des mythologies et des religions des sociétés traditionnelles et du monde antique, Flammarion, 1981.

ENGLISH TRANSLATIONS OF WORKS BY YVES BONNEFOY:

On the Motion and Immobility of Douve, tr. Galway Kinnell, Ohio University Press, 1968.

Selected Poems, tr. Anthony Rudolf, Jonathan Cape, 1968 (Grossman, 1969).

Rimbaud, tr. Paul Schmidt, Harper and Row, 1973.

Words in Stone/Pierre écrite, tr. Susanna Lang, University of Massachusetts Press, 1976.

The Origin of Language and Other Poems, with etchings by George Nama, tr. Susanna Lang, Monument Press, 1979.

Things Dying Things Newborn: Selected Poems, tr. Anthony Rudolf, The Menard Press, 1985.

Poems 1959–1975, tr. Richard Pevear, Random House, 1985.

Les Raisins de Zeuxis et d'autres fables/The Grapes of Zeuxis and Other Fables, with etchings by George Nama, tr. Richard Stamelman, Monument Press, 1987.

The Act and the Place of Poetry, selected literary essays, tr. John Naughton, Richard Stamelman, Jean Stewart, Richard Pevear, et al., University of Chicago Press, 1989.

Encore les raisins de Zeuxis/Once More the Grapes of Zeuxis, with etchings by George Nama, tr. Richard Stamelman, Monument Press, 1990.

Early Poems (1947–1959), tr. Galway Kinnell and Richard Pevear, Ohio University Press, 1990.

In the Shadow's Light, tr. John Naughton, University of Chicago Press, 1991.

Edward Hopper, tr. Richard Stamelman, Tabard Press, 1991.

Mythologies, compiled by Yves Bonnefoy, tr. under the direction of Wendy Doniger, University of Chicago Press, 1991.

Alberto Giacometti: A Biography of His Work, tr. Jean Stewart, Abbeville Press, 1991.

Henri Cartier-Bresson, Photographer, tr. Richard Stamelman, Thames and Hudson, Bulfinch Press, 1992.

On the Motion and Immobility of Douve, tr. Galway Kinnell, Bloodaxe Books, 1992.

Derniers raisins de Zeuxis/The Last Grapes of Zeuxis, with ethings by George Nama, tr. Richard Stamelman, Monument Press, 1993.

Traité du pianiste, tr. Anthony Rudolf, The Delos Press, 1994.

The Lure and the Truth of Painting, selected essays on the visual arts, tr. by Richard Stamelman, John Naughton, Michael Sheringham, et al., University of Chicago Press, 1995.

WORKS ON YVES BONNEFOY PUBLISHED IN ENGLISH:

Mary Ann Caws, *Yves Bonnefoy,* Twayne Publishing Co., 1984.

John T. Naughton, *The Poetics of Yves Bonnefoy,* University of Chicago Press, 1984.

Richard Stamelman, *Lost beyond Telling: Representations of Death and Absence in Modern French Poetry,* Cornell University Press, 1990.

Jean-Jacques Thomas, *Concordance: Poems/by Yves Bonnefoy,* bilingual ed., Edwin Mellen Press, 1990.

SPECIAL ISSUES OF ENGLISH-LANGUAGE JOURNALS
DEVOTED TO YVES BONNEFOY:

An Homage to French Poet Yves Bonnefoy. World Literature Today, no. 53, Summer, 1979.

Modern Poetry in Translation, n.s., no. 1, Summer, 1992.

INDEX OF TITLES AND FIRST LINES